Vuex Quick Start Guide

Centralized State Management for your Vue.js applications

Andrea Koutifaris

BIRMINGHAM - MUMBAI

Vuex Quick Start Guide

Commissioning Editors: Kunal Chaudhari
Acquisition Editor: Noyonika Das
Content Development Editors: Aditi Gour
Technical Editor: Sushmeeta Jena
Copy Editor: Safis Editing
Project Coordinator: Hardik Bhinde
Proofreader: Safis Editing
Indexers: Pratik Shirodkar
Graphics: Jason Monteiro
Production Coordinator: Aparna Bhagat

First published: April 2018

Production reference: 2050418

Published by Packt Publishing Ltd.
Livery Place
35 Livery Street
Birmingham
B3 2PB, UK.

ISBN 978-1-78899-993-9

www.packtpub.com

`mapt.io`

Mapt is an online digital library that gives you full access to over 5,000 books and videos, as well as industry leading tools to help you plan your personal development and advance your career. For more information, please visit our website.

Why subscribe?

- Spend less time learning and more time coding with practical eBooks and Videos from over 4,000 industry professionals

- Improve your learning with Skill Plans built especially for you

- Get a free eBook or video every month

- Mapt is fully searchable

- Copy and paste, print, and bookmark content

PacktPub.com

Did you know that Packt offers eBook versions of every book published, with PDF and ePub files available? You can upgrade to the eBook version at `www.PacktPub.com` and as a print book customer, you are entitled to a discount on the eBook copy. Get in touch with us at `service@packtpub.com` for more details.

At `www.PacktPub.com`, you can also read a collection of free technical articles, sign up for a range of free newsletters, and receive exclusive discounts and offers on Packt books and eBooks.

Contributors

About the author

Andrea Koutifaris has a passion for programming, which he likes to say is in his DNA. At the age of thirteen, he began using his father's laptop to write his own programs. After graduating high school, he enrolled, without a second thought, at the University of Florence, Faculty of Computer Engineering. After being a Java developer for some years, Andrea gradually moved to frontend development, which is still his passion today. Having spent too much time fixing problems with messed up code, he is obsessed with good programming and test-driven development which, in his opinion, is the only way to write production-quality code.

To the people who helped me during the creation of this book, in no particular order: Aditi Gour, Noyonika Das, Luca Martini, Francesco Strazzullo, and the other reviewers. To my beloved wife, who took up extra work so that I could write this book, and to my parents, who helped me a lot with important matters in my life.

About the reviewer

Francesco Strazzullo is a frontend engineer and trainer for E-xtrategy. He loves to share what he learns in his job by writing on his blog or presenting some new talk at a conference or some local JavaScript user group. During his free time, he likes to relax by playing with his PlayStation or cooking.

Bogdan, a tech lead with a passion for UI technologies, has worked with JavaScript for the past 12 years, from the emergence of jQuery and Ajax to state-of-the-art solutions such as React, Angular, Ember.js, and Vue.js. When not fiddling with some new coding challenge, he spends his time watching sports or movies with friends and family.

Nowadays he channels most of his efforts into making we3interactive one of the most successful and creative startups in Cluj.

His passion for Vue.js pushed him to collaborate on great books such as *Learning Vue.js*, *Vue.js 2 Cookbook*, and *Vue.js by Example*.

Packt is searching for authors like you

If you're interested in becoming an author for Packt, please visit `authors.packtpub.com` and apply today. We have worked with thousands of developers and tech professionals, just like you, to help them share their insight with the global tech community. You can make a general application, apply for a specific hot topic that we are recruiting an author for, or submit your own idea.

Table of Contents

Preface

Vuex is a centralized state management architecture for building client-side web applications. It exploits the Vue.js reactivity system to perfectly integrate into Vue.js applications.

In this book, you will understand why centralized state management is important, how it works, and how you can empower your Vue.js applications with Vuex. Finally, you will learn about the Vuex plugin system and use it to enrich your Vuex applications.

Who this book is for

This book targets Vue.js developers who want to understand and use Vuex centralized state management architecture in their applications.

What this book covers

Chapter 1, *Rethinking User Interfaces with Flux, Vue, and Vuex*, introduces the concepts of Flux architecture and the small differences in Vuex implementation.

Chapter 2, *Implementing Flux Architecture with Vuex*, teaches the core concepts of Vuex, and we learn how we can use them with small executable examples.

Chapter 3, *Setting Up Development and Test Environment*, shows how to use webpack and npm to prepare our environment for developing and testing a Vue/Vuex application.

Chapter 4, *Coding the EveryNote App Using Vuex State Management*, explains how to develop an application to take notes, using all the concepts from Vuex we've just learned. In addition, we use karma to test all the components of the application.

Chapter 5, *Debugging Vuex Applications*, says that even by testing every component, sometimes debugging is necessary. We will understand how to use Chrome Developer tools and vue-devtools to debug our applications.

Chapter 6, *Using the Vuex Plugin System*, enriches the EveryNote app with some useful Vuex plugins, including two custom plugins developed from scratch.

To get the most out of this book

In this book, we assume that the reader has good knowledge of the Vue.js framework, a good knowledge of JavaScript, and basic knowledge of EcmaScript 6.

In addition, to run the examples, the reader needs to install Node.js and have a very basic understanding of **node package manager** (**npm**).

Finally, to use the Git repository of this book, the user needs to install Git and have a basic understanding of Git commands.

Download the example code files

You can download the example code files for this book from your account at www.packtpub.com. If you purchased this book elsewhere, you can visit www.packtpub.com/support and register to have the files emailed directly to you.

You can download the code files by following these steps:

1. Log in or register at www.packtpub.com.
2. Select the **SUPPORT** tab.
3. Click on **Code Downloads & Errata**.
4. Enter the name of the book in the **Search** box and follow the onscreen instructions.

Once the file is downloaded, please make sure that you unzip or extract the folder using the latest version of:

- WinRAR/7-Zip for Windows
- Zipeg/iZip/UnRarX for Mac
- 7-Zip/PeaZip for Linux

The code bundle for the book is also hosted on GitHub at https://github.com/PacktPublishing/Vuex-Quick-Start-Guide. We also have other code bundles from our rich catalog of books and videos available at https://github.com/PacktPublishing/. Check them out!

Download the color images

We also provide a PDF file that has color images of the screenshots/diagrams used in this book. You can download it here: `https://www.packtpub.com/sites/default/files/downloads/VuexQuickStartGuide_ColorImages`.

Code in Action

Visit the following link to check out videos of the code being run:
`https://goo.gl/8WLxhs`

Conventions used

There are a number of text conventions used throughout this book.

`CodeInText`: Indicates code words in text, database table names, folder names, filenames, file extensions, pathnames, dummy URLs, user input, and Twitter handles. Here is an example: "Mount the downloaded `WebStorm-10*.dmg` disk image file as another disk in your system."

A block of code is set as follows:

```
html, body, #map {
  height: 100%;
  margin: 0;
  padding: 0
}
```

When we wish to draw your attention to a particular part of a code block, the relevant lines or items are set in bold:

```
[default]
exten => s,1,Dial(Zap/1|30)
exten => s,2,Voicemail(u100)
exten => s,102,Voicemail(b100)
exten => i,1,Voicemail(s0)
```

Any command-line input or output is written as follows:

```
$ mkdir css
$ cd css
```

Bold: Indicates a new term, an important word, or words that you see onscreen. For example, words in menus or dialog boxes appear in the text like this. Here is an example: "Select **System info** from the **Administration** panel."

 Warnings or important notes appear like this.

 Tips and tricks appear like this.

Get in touch

Feedback from our readers is always welcome.

General feedback: Email `feedback@packtpub.com` and mention the book title in the subject of your message. If you have questions about any aspect of this book, please email us at `questions@packtpub.com`.

Errata: Although we have taken every care to ensure the accuracy of our content, mistakes do happen. If you have found a mistake in this book, we would be grateful if you would report this to us. Please visit `www.packtpub.com/submit-errata`, selecting your book, clicking on the Errata Submission Form link, and entering the details.

Piracy: If you come across any illegal copies of our works in any form on the Internet, we would be grateful if you would provide us with the location address or website name. Please contact us at `copyright@packtpub.com` with a link to the material.

If you are interested in becoming an author: If there is a topic that you have expertise in and you are interested in either writing or contributing to a book, please visit `authors.packtpub.com`.

Reviews

Please leave a review. Once you have read and used this book, why not leave a review on the site that you purchased it from? Potential readers can then see and use your unbiased opinion to make purchase decisions, we at Packt can understand what you think about our products, and our authors can see your feedback on their book. Thank you!

For more information about Packt, please visit packtpub.com.

1
Rethinking User Interfaces with Flux, Vue, and Vuex

I started my first job as a Java EE programmer at the end of 2007. I still remember my friend Giuseppe saying, *You don't like JavaScript, do you?* and me answering, *No, I don't. Each time I write something in JavaScript, it doesn't work in all versions of Internet Explorer... not to mention Firefox!* He just replied, *Have a look at jQuery.* Today, I like to call myself a JavaScript programmer.

Since then, web development has evolved a lot. A number of JavaScript frameworks became popular and then declined because new frameworks emerged. You may think that it is not worth learning new frameworks since they will eventually decline in popularity. Well, in my opinion, that is not true. Each framework added something useful to web development, something that we still use. For example, jQuery made use of JavaScript that was so simple that we started moving client logic to the browser instead of rendering everything server-side.

Today, we write progressive web applications that are complex applications with web user interfaces. This complexity requires discipline and best practices. Fortunately, big companies such as Facebook, Google, and others have introduced frameworks and guidelines to help web programmers. You may have heard about Google's *Material Design* or Facebook's *Flux*.

In this chapter we will focus on the following:

- **Model-view-controller** (**MVC**) problems, and using Facebook Flux architecture to solve these problems
- Flux fundamentals
- What Vuex is
- Architectural differences between Flux and Vuex

To understand this book, you need a good knowledge of Vue.js and JavaScript, a basic understanding of ECMAScript 6, and a very basic knowledge of webpack. In any case, almost all the concepts used here, Vuex and otherwise, are explained.

After explaining the Flux concepts, this book will help you understand how Vuex implements these concepts, how to use Vue.js and Vuex to build professional web applications, and finally how to extend Vuex functionality.

MVC problems and the Flux solution

Each time we speak about an application with a user interface, the MVC pattern comes out. But what is the MVC pattern? It is an architectural pattern that divides components into three parts: a **Model**, a **View**, and a **Controller**. You can see the classic diagram describing MVC in the following figure:

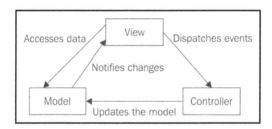

Figure 1.0: Classic MVC diagram

Most of the modern frameworks for progressive web applications use the MVC pattern. In fact, if you look at the Vue.js single file component shown in the following figure, you can clearly see the three parts of the MVC pattern:

```
V Hello.vue ×
1   <template>
2     <p>{{greeting}} World!</p>
3   </template>
4
5   <script>
6     const HelloController = {
7       data() {
8         return {
9           greeting: 'Hello'
10         };
11       }
12     };
13
14     export default HelloController;
15   </script>
16
17   <style lang="scss" scoped>
18     p {
19       font-family: "Arial Rounded MT", Arial, sans-serif;
20     }
21   </style>
```

Figure 1.1: Vue.js single file component

The `template` and `style` parts represent the view section, the `script` part provides the controller, and the `data` section of the controller is the model.

But what happens when we need some data from the model of a component that's inside another component? Moreover, in general, how can we interconnect all the components of a page?

Clearly, providing direct access to the model of the components from other components is not a good idea. The following screenshot shows the dependencies in the case of exposing the models:

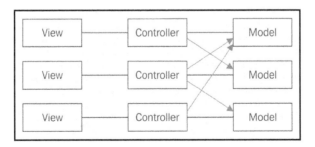

Figure 1.2: MVC hell

Vue.js provides a good way of communicating between parent and child components: You can use *Props* to pass values from a parent to a child component, and you can *emit* data from a child component to its parent. The following figure shows a visual representation of this concept:

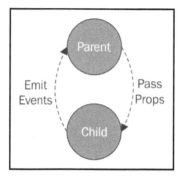

Figure 1.3: Vue.js parent–child communication

However, when multiple components share a common state, this way of communicating is not enough. The following are the issues that would come up:

- Multiple views may share the same piece of state
- User actions from different views may need to change the same piece of state

Some frameworks provide a component called `EventBus`; in fact, the Vue instance itself is an `EventBus`. It has two methods: `Vue.$emit(event, [eventData])` and `Vue.$on(event, callback([eventData]))`. The following is an example of how to create a global event bus:

```
// EventBus.js
import Vue from 'vue';
export const EventBus = new Vue();

// HelloWorldEmitter.js
import { EventBus } from './EventBus.js';
EventBus.$emit('an-event', 'Hello world');

// HelloWorldReceiver.js
import { EventBus } from './EventBus.js';
EventBus.$on('an-event', eventData => {
 console.log(eventData);
});
```

Even with a global event bus, making components communicate is not easy. What if a component that registers to an event gets loaded after the event is fired? It will miss the event. This may happen if that component is inside a module that gets loaded later, which is likely to happen in a progressive web app where modules are lazily loaded.

For example, say that a user wants to add a product to the cart list. She taps on the **Add to cart** button, which is likely to be in the `CartList` component, and she expects the product she sees on the screen to be saved in the cart. How can the `CartList` component find out what the product is that should be added to its list?

Well, it seems that Facebook programmers faced similar problems, and to solve those problems, they designed what they called *Flux*: Application architecture for building user interfaces.

Inspired by Flux and Elm architecture, Evan You, the author of *Vue.js*, created Vuex. You may know Redux already. In that case, you will find that Vuex and Redux are similar, and that Evan You saved us time by implementing Vuex instead of forcing every programmer to integrate Redux inside a Vue.js application. In addition, Vuex is designed around Vue.js to provide the best integration between the two frameworks.

But what is Vuex? That is the topic of the next section.

What is Vuex?

Evan You defines Vuex as:

> *"state management pattern + library for Vue.js applications. It serves as a centralized store for all the components in an application, with rules ensuring that the state can only be mutated in a predictable fashion."*

Without knowing Flux, this definition sounds a little bit obscure. Actually, Vuex is a Flux implementation that exploits the reactivity system of Vue using a single, centralized store, and ensures that *the state can only be mutated in a predictable fashion*.

Before focusing on Vuex itself, we are going to understand the fundamentals of Flux and how Vuex took inspiration from these concepts.

Understanding the Flux fundamentals

Flux is a pattern for managing data flow in your application, and it is the application architecture that Facebook uses for building its web applications. The following diagram shows the structure and data flow in Flux:

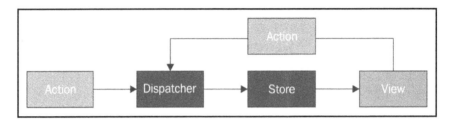

Figure 1.4: Structure and data flow in Flux

As shown in the preceding figure, Flux is divided into four parts, and *data flows in only one direction*. In the next sections, we will see how data flows through the following parts:

- Actions
- Dispatchers
- Stores
- Views

Although it is important to understand how Flux works, Vuex has its own implementation of Flux architecture that differs from Flux, and it will be explained in detail in the following chapters.

Actions

Actions define the internal API of your application. They represent what can be done, but not how it is done. The logic of state mutation is contained inside stores. An action is simply an object with a type and some data.

Actions should be meaningful to the reader and they should avoid implementation details. For example, `remove-product-from-cart` is better than splitting it into `update-server-cart`, `refresh-cart-list`, and `update-money-total`.

An action is dispatched to all the stores and it can cause more than one store to update. So dispatching an action will result in one or more stores executing the corresponding action handler.

For example, when a user taps on the **Remove from cart** button, a `remove-product-from-cart` action is dispatched:

```
{type: 'remove-product-from-cart', productID: '21'}
```

In Vuex, the action system is a bit different, and it splits Flux actions into two concepts:

- Actions
- Mutations

Actions represent a behavior of an application, something that the application must do. The result of an action consists typically of one or more mutations being committed. Committing a mutation means executing its associated handler. It is not possible to change the Vuex state directly inside an action; instead, actions commit mutations.

You have to deal with asynchronous code inside actions, since mutations must be synchronous.

Mutations, on the other hand, can and do modify the application state. They represent the application logic directly connected to the application state. Mutations should be simple, since complex behavior should be handled by actions.

Since there is only one store in Vuex, actions are dispatched using the store, and there is a direct connection between an action and its handler. In Flux, on the other hand, every store knows what to do when responding to the action.

You will read about the Vuex action/mutation system in the following chapters. Right now, you just need to understand the concepts behind actions, and that Vuex implements actions in a slightly different way than the one used by Flux.

Dispatcher

There is only one dispatcher per application, and it receives actions and dispatches them to the stores. Every store receives every action. It is a simple mechanism to dispatch actions, and it can handle dependencies between stores by dispatching actions to the stores in a specific order.

For example:

1. A user taps on the **Add to cart** button
2. The view captures this event and dispatches an `add-to-cart` action
3. Every store receives this action

Since Vuex differs from Flux because the dispatcher is inside the store, what you should remember here is that every change in the application begins by dispatching an action.

Stores

Stores contain the application state and logic. Stores can be mutated only by actions and do not expose any setter method. There can be more than one store in Flux, each one representing a domain within the application. In Vuex, there is only one store, and its state is called a single state tree. Vuex is not the only framework that enforces the use of a single store: Redux explicitly states that there is one store per Redux application. You may think that a single store may break modularity. We will see later how modularity works on Vuex.

Before switching to Flux architecture, Facebook chat kept experiencing a bug where the number of unread messages was wrong. Instead of having two lists—one of read messages and another of unread ones—they used to derive the number of unread messages from other components events. It is indeed better to have an explicit state where all the information is stored. Think of the state as an application snapshot: You could save it before the application page gets closed and restore it when the application gets opened again so that the user will find the application in the same state it was left in.

There are three important concepts regarding stores:

- Stores can be mutated only by actions
- Once a store is mutated, it notifies it has changed to the views
- Stores represent explicit data, as opposed to deriving data from events

Here is an example of a store reacting to the `add-to-cart` action dispatched in the previous example:

1. The store receives the `add-to-cart` action
2. It decides it is relevant and executes the logic of the action by adding the current product to the cart product list
3. It updates its data and then notifies the views that it has changed

Views

Views, or view controllers, display data from the stores. Here is where a framework like Vue.js plugs in.

Rendering data in the stores

In the Facebook video introducing Flux, software engineer Jing Chen talks about some of the problems they faced while developing Facebook Chat, and what lessons they learned. One interesting lesson they learned concerns rendering: They didn't want to rerender all the messages in the chat, but instead wanted to optimize it a bit by updating the chat view with only the new messages. If you are an experienced programmer, you may think, *This is a premature optimization*. Indeed it is! It is much more simple to pass the whole view-model to the views rather than just pass the differences from the old and new model.

Say that a programmer wants to add a new feature to a view: If the view-model is rendered by the view each time it is modified, they just need to add some properties to the model and add some code to the view to display these new properties. They don't need to worry about updating/rendering logic.

But what about performance? Isn't it bad to rerender the whole page just because the number of unread messages has changed? Here, Vue.js comes to help us. A programmer just needs to update the view-model and Vue.js will understand what has changed and will rerender only the **Document Object Model (DOM)** parts that actually changed. The following diagram schematizes this concept:

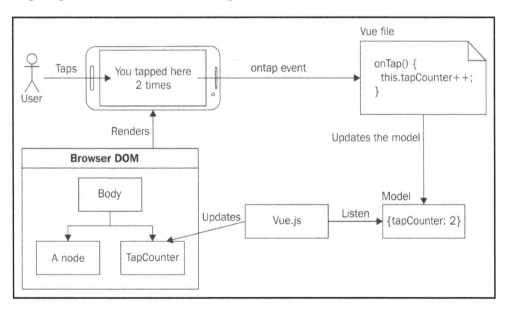

Figure 1.5: Vue.js updating a DOM node

The lesson is this: Spend time on designing explicit, meaningful models and let Vue.js take care of the performance and rendering logic.

 The **DOM** is used to render a web page. See `https://www.w3schools.com/js/js_htmldom.asp` for more information.

Stores and private components model

Since views display data from stores, you may think that a view-model is just a portion of a store. Actually, each component can have a private model that can hold values that are needed just inside the component. There is no need to put every value in a store. Stores should contain only data relevant to the application.

For example, say you want to select some photos from a list and share them. The view-model of the photo list component will contain the list of selected photos, and when a user taps on the **Share** button, the view-controller just needs to dispatch an action called `share-photos` with the selected photo list as data in the `action` object. There is no need to put the selected photo list inside a store.

Summarizing Flux architecture

The following is the Flux architecture summarized in a single image:

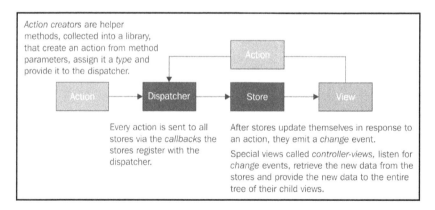

Figure 1.6: Flux data flow explained

Benefits of using Flux

The following are some of the benefits that Facebook gained after introducing Flux to their web applications:

- Better scalability than the classic MVC
- Easy-to-understand data flow
- Easier and more effective unit tests
- Since actions represent behaviors of the application, behavior-driven development is a perfect match to write applications using Flux architecture

By adding the Vuex framework to your Vue.js application, you will experience the same benefits. In addition, Vuex, like Redux, simplified this architecture in several different ways, such as using a single store per application and removing the dispatcher from the process in favor of using the store to dispatch actions.

Summary

In this chapter, we looked at why Facebook engineers designed the Flux architecture. We focused on the fundamentals of Flux and learned that Vuex differs slightly from Flux. We can now summarize Flux in one sentence: Flux is a predictable state management system with a one-way data flow.

In Chapter 2, *Implementing Flux Architecture with Vuex*, you will learn the core concepts of Vuex, as well as how you can use Vuex in your applications.

Implementing Flux Architecture with Vuex

2

With the Flux concepts clear in our minds, we will now explore the Vuex framework, understand how it works, and, with the help of some examples, see how you can use Vuex inside your Vue applications.

This chapter will cover the following topics:

- Vuex at a glance
- The boilerplate code that will be used to run the examples
- The Vue.js reactivity system explained
- Understanding the core concepts of Vuex
- Enabling strict mode while developing to prevent accidental direct state modifications
- Restrictions in form handling when using Vuex
- Simple counter: all the Vuex concepts in a very simple example

The first section introduces you to Vuex, focusing on the concepts behind the framework.

In the second section, you will be presented with a minimal HTML code to run the examples in this chapter.

In the third section, the Vue reactivity system is examined in detail. This is useful because Vuex exploits this reactivity system to plug itself seemlessly into the Vue application's architecture.

In the fourth section, all Vuex core concepts are thoroughly examined, and, with the help of code snippets, you will see that Vuex is both powerful and simple to use.

The fifth and sixth sections will explain some concepts to keep in mind when using Vuex inside your applications.

Finally, in the last part of this chapter, a simple example will show you most of the Vuex concepts put together in a single HTML file, helping you to understand the whole picture.

Once you have read this chapter, you will have a clear understanding of the Vuex framework, and you will be ready to start using it.

Technical requirements

You will be required to have Node.js installed on a system. Finally, to use the Git repository of this book, the user needs to install Git.

The code files of this chapter can be found on GitHub:
`https://github.com/PacktPublishing/Vuex-Quick-Start-Guide/tree/master/chapter-2`

Check out the following video to see the code in action:
`https://goo.gl/2zXEav`

Vuex at a glance

In `Chapter 1`, *Rethinking User Interfaces with Flux, Vue and Vuex*, we defined Vuex as *a state management pattern + library for Vue.js applications. It serves as a centralized store for all the components in an application, with rules ensuring that the state can only be mutated in a predictable fashion.*

Although I think that, having read `Chapter 1`, *Rethinking User Interfaces with Flux, Vue and* definition should sound clear enough to you, it is still a bit obscure. Let's list down the three concepts contained in the preceding sentences:

- The centralized store
- The fact that the state can only be mutated in a predictable way
- The Vue reactivity system

If you look back to *Figure 1.6* in *Flux architecture summarized* section in `Chapter 1`, *Rethinking User Interfaces with Flux, Vue and Vuex*, you will see that the Flux architecture has one dispatcher that dispatches actions to every store. Having only one store means that the dispatcher can be inside the store and you can dispatch actions using the centralized store. In Vuex, we have a single store and its state is called **single state tree**.

One fundamental rule in Flux and Vuex is that the state can be mutated only because of an action. No component, class, or piece of code should modify the state. Only the code that is linked to an action can actually change the state values. this by using mutations that can only be executed by actions. In this, Vuex differs from Flux. In Flux, actions are just data objects containing the information about the action to be performed. In Vuex, actions can execute code that will eventually end by committing one or more mutations that will change the state. You will read about mutations and actions later in this chapter.

Finally, after an action has been dispatched and the state has been updated, it must notify the views of the application of the fact that has changed. This is done by taking advantage of the Vue reactivity system, which is the topic of the next section.

Boilerplate code for the examples

In the next few pages, you will be provided with some examples. In order to execute these examples, you need to create an HTML file as follows:

```
<!DOCTYPE html>
<html lang="en">
<head>
  <meta charset="UTF-8">
  <title>Vuex condensed example</title>
</head>
<body>
<div id="app"></div>
<script src="https://unpkg.com/vuex@3.0.1/dist/vuex.min.js"></script>
<script src="https://unpkg.com/vue@2.5.13/dist/vue.min.js"></script>
<script>
  Vue.use(Vuex);
 // Add code from examples here
</script>
</body>
</html>
```

By copying the example code inside the `<script>` tag, you can run it and see the results. Almost every example code can be found in the Git repository of this book, under the `/chapter-2/` folder.

Vue.js reactivity system explained

One of the powerful features of Vue is its reactivity system. It is an unobtrusive way to detect changes to the components model. A component model is just a plain JavaScript object. When it changes, Vue detects the changes and updates the corresponding views. In Vuex, the single state tree is reactive, like the data part of a Vue component.

It is important to understand how the reactivity system works to avoid some common mistakes.

There are two ways to detect whether a value inside a JavaScript object has changed:

- By using the Proxy feature, which is defined in ECMAScript 2015 (6th Edition, ECMA-262)
- By using Object.defineProperty, which is defined in ECMAScript 2011 (5.1 Edition, ECMA-262)

For compatibility reasons, Vue decided to use Object.defineProperty, which means that there are some limitations.

When you create a component, Vue will walk through all the properties of the data part and use Object.defineProperty to convert them into getter/setter methods. For this reason, Vue can only detect changes to properties that have been defined in the data part of a component. Let's see an example:

```
// Bugged example of counter
Vue.use(Vuex);
const CounterComponent = {
  template: `
  <div>
   <p>I will count from 1 to {{end}}.</p>
   <button @click="beginCounting">Begin!</button>
   <p>{{counter}}</p>
  </div>
  `,
  created() {
    this.counter = 0;
  },
  data() {
    return {
      end: 3,
      // you should add counter property here
    };
  },
  methods: {
```

```
  beginCounting() {
    this.counter = 0;
    const increaseCounter = () => {
      this.counter++;
      if (this.counter < this.end) {
        setTimeout(increaseCounter, 1000);
      }
    };
    increaseCounter();
  },
  },
};

new Vue({
  el: '#app',
  template: '<counter></counter>',
  components: {
    counter: CounterComponent,
  },
});
```

In this example, the `counter` property is not declared in the `data` section of the component. This prevents Vue from detecting that `counter` has been changed, and so, when a user clicks on the button **Begin!**, they will not see the counter increasing.

This can be easily fixed by adding `counter` to the `data` section and removing it from the `created()` method. Look at the following code:

```
data() {
  return {
      end: 3,
      counter: 0
  };
},
```

You can find the code for the preceding example in the Git repository of this book, inside the file `chapter-2/counterTo3/counter.html`.

When using `Arrays`, Vue cannot detect the following changes:

- Setting a value directly using the index—for example, `this.items[indexOfItem] = newItem`
- Changing the array length—for example, `this.items.length = newLength`

To avoid these problems, you could either create a new array and assign it to the corresponding data property, or use array methods, such as `push()` or `splice()`. The following are different ways to update an array observed by Vue:

```
// Replacing the array
this.items[1] = updatedItem;
this.items = this.items.slice();

// Using splice to change element at index 1
this.items.splice(1,1,updatedItem);

// Adding a new item
this.items.push(newItem);
```

We now understood that every time we properly change something inside a component model or inside the single state tree, Vue detects it and updates the corresponding views accordingly. But what about performance? Isn't it bad to update the views on each modification? In fact, Vue exploits how the JavaScript event loop works to queue all the updates to the views. To understand this concept, let's focus on the following example:

```
console.log('start');
Promise.resolve().then(() => console.log('promise'));
setTimeout(() => console.log('timeout'), 0);
console.log('end')
```

The expected output (which may vary on different browsers) is:

```
start
end
promise
timeout
```

First, the JavaScript virtual machine executes the synchronous code that prints `start` and `end`, then it executes all the jobs queued during the execution, printing `promise` and `timeout`.

Vue uses `Promise` if it is available on the user browser; otherwise, it tries to find the best scheduling function, with a fallback to `setTimeout` in case no other supported scheduling function has been found. Today, `Promise` is supported in almost every browser, mobile, and desktop.

Understanding the core concepts of Vuex

It is now time to introduce the Vuex architecture, which consists of five core concepts:

- Single state tree
- Getters
- Mutations
- Actions
- Modules

Each concept will be discussed in detail, with some pieces of code that will help to make it clear. Once you have read the following pages, you will have a clear understanding of Vuex architecture.

Understanding the Vuex store

Vuex implements Flux stores using a single state tree. In this, it differs from Flux because in Flux there could be more than one store. You may think that a single store/state is not good for modularity. Later, we will see how to split the single state tree into modules.

Having only one store has some benefits:

- It is available in every component
- It is easier to debug since all the application state is there
- You can write unobstructive plugins that watch the state and perform an action, such as persisting the state for later retrieval

The single state tree contains all the application-level data—it represents the application domain model.

Accessing the single state tree inside components

Let's now see how to use this single state tree inside a Vue component using an example. Say that we want to show the number of unread messages in a chat session. Somewhere in the application, this number gets updated and the NumUnreadMessages component shows this number. The following is an example of how the component could be coded:

```
const NumUnreadMessages = {
  template: `<div>Unread: {{ unreadCounter }}</div>`,
  computed: {
```

```
    unreadCounter() {
      return this.$store.state.unreadCounter;
    },
  },
};
```

As you can see, it is straightforward—you just need to use `this.$store.state` to access the application state. In order to have `this.$store` available inside Vue `components`, you need to add the store to the `Vue` application:

```
Vue.use(Vuex);
const store = new Vuex.Store({
  state: {
    unreadCounter: 1,
  },
});

const NumUnreadMessages = {
  template: `<div>Unread: {{ unreadCounter }}</div>`,
  computed: {
    unreadCounter() {
      return this.$store.state.unreadCounter;
    },
  },
};

const app = new Vue({
  el: '#app',
  store,
  components: {NumUnreadMessages},
  template: `
  <div class="app">
    <num-unread-messages></num-unread-messages>
  </div>
  `,
});
```

You can find the code for this example in the Git repository of this book, inside the file `chapter-2/unread-messages/unread.html`.

The mapState helper

Creating a computed property every time we want to access the state could be tedious and verbose, especially if a component needs more than one state property.

Fortunately, Vuex provides a handy tool called `mapState`:

```
const NumUnreadMessages = {
  // ...
  computed: Vuex.mapState({
      unreadCounter: state => state.unreadCounter,
  })
}
```

In the preceding code, the computed property `unreadCounter` is mapped to `this.$store.state.unreadCounter`. Since `mapState` is not well documented, I am going to explain all the ways that you can use it.

- You can use functions, as shown in the following code:

```
// Using functions with mapState
 const NumUnreadMessages = {
   data() {
     return {label:' unread messages'};
   },
   computed: mapState({
     unreadCounter: state => state.unreadCounter,
     unreadCounterPlusLabel(state) {
       // Here you can use this keyword to access
       // the local state of the component.
       return state.unreadCounter + this.label;
     }
   })
 }
```

`unreadCounter` is an arrow function, whereas `unreadCounterAlias` is a normal function. If you want to access the local state of the component, you must use a function and not an arrow function; otherwise, you cannot use the `this` keyword inside the arrow function.

- You can use `strings`, as shown in the following code snippet:

```
// Using strings
computed: mapState({
  // Equivalent to unreadCounter: state => state.unreadCounter
  unreadCounter: 'unreadCounter'
})
```

- Finally, there is a much more concise way that can be used if the name of the state property and the name of the computed property are the same:

```
// Using string array
computed: mapState([
  // map this.unreadCounter to store.state.unreadCounter
  'unreadCounter'
])
```

In this case, you just need to pass an array of strings to mapState, where each string is the name of the state property you want to map.

You may wonder how you can mix local computed properties with the ones coming from mapState. Here is an example using the ECMAScript 6 object spread operator:

```
computed: {
  localComputed () {
    // returning localProperty declared into data section
    return this.localProperty;
  },
  ...mapState([
    'unreadCounter'
  ])
}
```

The use of the ES6 object spread operator . . . is not yet commonly known among programmers, especially when used with objects. See the following example if this operator sounds new to you:

```
const obj = {b:'b', c:'c'};
console.log({a:'a', ...obj , d:'d'});
// prints {a: "a", b: "b", c: "c", d: "d"}
```

Components' local state

Even if there is a global single state tree, it doesn't mean that components cannot have a local state. What is in the global state is application-wide and should not be polluted with the component's private state. For example, text parts of a component are likely to be used only inside the component, and for this reason, they should not be put into the application state.

Computing a derived state with getters

Sometimes two or more components need a derived state based on the values inside the state. You could compute the derived state inside every component, but this means duplicating code, which is not acceptable. To avoid this, you could create an external function or utility class to compute the derived state, which is better than duplicating the code. However, Vuex provides getter functions so that we can write derived state code inside the application store, avoiding all these unnecessary steps.

For example, say that the app state contains a list of messages, and, when a new message is added to that list, it gets marked as unread. We could then write a getter function that returns all the unread messages:

```
const store = new Vuex.Store({
  state: {
    messages: [
      { id: 1, text: 'First message', read: true },
      { id: 2, text: 'Second message', read: false },
    ],
  },
  getters: {
    unreadMessages(state) {
      return state.messages.filter(message => !message.read);
    },
  },
});
```

A getter function also receives all the getters as the second argument:

```
getters: {
  // ...
  unreadCounter(state, getters) => {
    return getters.unreadMessages.length;
  }
}
```

We can now update the unread messages example using getter functions:

```
Vue.use(Vuex);
const store = new Vuex.Store({
  state: {
    messages: [
      { id: 1, text: 'First message', read: true },
      { id: 2, text: 'Second message', read: false },
    ],
  },
```

```
getters: {
  unreadMessages(state) {
    return state.messages.filter(message => !message.read);
  },
  unreadCounter(state, getters) {
    return getters.unreadMessages.length;
  },
},
});

const NumUnreadMessages = {
  template: `<div>Unread: {{ unreadCounter }}</div>`,
  computed: {
    unreadCounter() {
      return this.$store.getters.unreadCounter;
    },
  },
};

new Vue({
  el: '#app',
  store,
  components: { NumUnreadMessages },
  template: `
  <div class="app">
    <num-unread-messages></num-unread-messages>
  </div>
  `,
});
```

You will find the code for the following example in the Git repository of this book, inside the file named `chapter-2/unread-messages/unread-with-getters.html`.

`Getter` functions can also receive parameters, making them useful when executing queries regarding the state. To receive parameters, the `getter` functions must return a function that receives the parameters. Look at the following example:

```
getters: {
  // ...
  getMessageById(state) {
    return (id) => {
      return state.messages.find(msg => msg.id === id);
    }
  }
}
```

As for the state, there is a `mapState` helper. For getters, there is a `mapGetters` helper.

The mapGetters helper

The `mapGetters` helper simply maps store `getters` to local computed properties. :

```
const NumUnreadMessages = {
  template: `<div>Unread: {{ unreadCounter }}</div>`,
  computed: Vuex.mapGetters(['unreadCounter']),
};
```

As for `mapState`, we can use an array to list all the `getters` properties we want to map to a corresponding computed property.

If the name of the computed property is different from the `getter` name, you can use an object instead of an array:

```
...mapGetters({
  // map `this.numUnread` to `store.getters.unreadCounter`
  numUnread: 'unreadCounter'
```

You will find the code for this updated example of unread messages in the Git repository of this book, inside the file named `chapter-2/unread-messages/unread-with-getters-and-mapgetters.html`.

Changing the application state with mutations

Until now, we have only seen how the app state can be retrieved. It is time to introduce mutations. Using mutations is the only way you can change the state. If you remember, Flux only allows actions to mutate the state. In Vuex, actions are split into actions and mutations. We will introduce actions later—here, we will focus on mutations and how we can change the state using Vuex.

In order to change the state, you need to commit a mutation. A mutation is similar to an event: you declare the mutation, which is a kind of event type, and link the mutation to a piece of code, which is like an event handler. From this point of view, Vuex can be seen as an evolution of the `EventBus` pattern, which was discussed in `Chapter 1`, *Rethinking User Interfaces with Flux, Vue and Vuex*, as a possible solution to let MVC components communicate with each other.

Mutations are declared in the `mutations` section of the `config` object provided to the `Vuex.Store(...)` function:

```
const store = new Vuex.Store({
  state: {
    messages: []
  },
  mutations: {
    addNewMessage (state, msgText) {
      // mutating the state
      state.messages.push({text: msgText, read: false});
    }
  }
})
```

Commiting a mutation

You cannot call a mutation handler directly. Instead, you can commit the mutation using `store.commit(mutationName, payload)`. For example:

```
store.commit('addNewMessage', 'A message');
```

This will add a message to the `messages` array of the application state.

The `payload` parameter can be a primitive type or an object with all the properties that the mutation needs.

You can also use an object-style commit, as shown in the following example:

```
store.commit({
  type: 'addNewMessage',
  content: 'A message'
});
```

Since with a mutation you change the state that is reactive, it is recommended that you follow some best practices:

- Initialize all the properties of the state so that they represent the initial state of the application
- Ensure that when you modify or add a new property to the state, `Vue` will detect the modification, as discussed in the reactivity section of this chapter

The following is a complete example where a user can add a message and see the message list:

```
Vue.use(Vuex);
const store = new Vuex.Store({
  state: {
    messages: [],
  },
  mutations: {
    addNewMessage(state, msgText) {
      state.messages.push({ text: msgText, read: false });
    },
  },
});

const MessageList = {
  template: `<ul>
      <li v-for="message in messages">{{message.text}}</li>
    </ul>
  `,
  computed: Vuex.mapState(['messages']),
};

const MessageEditor = {
  template: `<div>
    <input type="text" v-model="message">
    <button @click="addMessage">Add message</button>
  </div>
  `,
  data() {
    return {
      message: '',
    };
  },
  methods: {
    addMessage() {
      this.$store.commit('addNewMessage', this.message);
    },
  },
};

new Vue({
  el: '#app',
  store,
  components: { MessageList, MessageEditor },
  template: `
  <div class="app">
```

```
    <message-editor></message-editor>
    <message-list></message-list>
  </div>
  `,
});
```

Enumerating mutation types using constant strings

Every time you want to commit a mutation, you need to write the type of mutation you want to perform. Scattering strings among the code is considered bad practice and has the following drawbacks:

- It is error-prone: typos or wrong casing could occur when typing the mutation type
- It is hard to rename a type, since you have to search for all the occurrences of that string in the code
- It is not clear which module that mutation comes from

For these reasons, it is better to use constant strings to define all the mutation types. Using uppercase will prevent wrong casing, and using constants variables will allow most editors to highlight occurrences. In addition, editors usually provide a way to rename variables, such as string constants, making it easy to rename a mutation.

Mutation types should be defined inside a file with all the possible mutations of the application, or of the module if the application is split into modules. In this way, it is easier to understand all the changes the application state can be subjected to. In fact, if you remember, Vuex promises that the state will be changed in a predictable fashion. Say that a new programmer participates in your project. You could sit next to them and start explaining what the application does. You will soon find out that they can understand what happens when a user performs an action without your help. In fact, they just need to follow the flow from the action fired inside a Vue component to the corresponding state mutation.

The following is an example illustrating how to use constant mutation types:

```
// mutation-types.js
export const ADD_NEW_MESSAGE = 'addNewMessage';

// store.js
import Vuex from 'vuex';
import { ADD_NEW_MESSAGE } from './mutation-types';

const store = new Vuex.Store({
  state: { ... },
```

```
  mutations: {
    [ADD_NEW_MESSAGE] (state, msgText) {
      state.messages.push({text: msgText, read: false});
    }
  }
});
```

Mutations must be synchronous

One important rule when using Vuex is that *mutation handler functions must be synchronous*.
Unfortunately, this cannot be enforced through JavaScript language, so Vuex cannot ensure
that you follow this rule. This means that this rule is a best practice that must be followed
when coding your application.

The following is an example that shows this rule being violated:

```
// Violation of rule "mutations handlers must be synchronous"
mutations: {
  updateBookDetailsById(state, partialBookData) {
    state.currentBook = partialBookData;
    const {bookId} = partialBookData;
    api.getBookDetailsById(bookId, (bookDetails) => {
      state.currentBook = bookDetails;
    });
  }
}
```

In this example, first `state.currentBook` is set with some partial data from the book,
then, when the server provides the requested book details, the `state.currentBook` state
gets updated with all the book details.

Showing book data as soon as possible is a good idea. We don't want the user to see a blank
page until the server provides all the requested information. But asynchronicity must be
dealt with somewhere else—more precisely, inside an `action`.

But what could happen in the preceding example? In the best case scenario, the book's
partial data is displayed and a few moments later, all the book details are shown. But
`api.getBookDetailsById(...)` could take longer than expected, or it can even fail. In
these last cases, the result will be an incoherent application state. What if
`state.currentBook` gets modified by the user before the server provides the book details?

To avoid these problems, when a mutation is committed, the application state must move
from a well-defined state to another well-defined state in a synchronous manner.

The mapMutations helper

As for the state and getters, there is a helper to save us some keystrokes.

The example, where a user can add a message, can be refactored using the mapMutations helper, as follows:

```
const MessageEditor = {
  template: `<div>
    <input type="text" v-model="message">
    <button @click="addNewMessage(message)">Add message</button>
  </div>
  `,
  data() {
    return {
      message: '',
    };
  },
  methods: Vuex.mapMutations([
    // Payload is also supported
    'addNewMessage'
  ]),
};
```

In this case, mapMutations(...) creates an addNewMessage method that calls this.$store.commit(ADD_NEW_MESSAGE, payload) when executed.

You will find the code for the preceding example with and without mapMutations inside the chapter-2/add-message folder.

Committing mutations within actions

As introduced earlier, Vuex splits Flux actions into mutations and actions. Mutations must be synchronous, so actions are where asynchronous code can be written. The idea is that mutations are well-defined state modifications and actions commit mutations to change the application state. For example, an action could request some data from the server, and when the server responds, commit a mutation using the data it just obtained.

In short, actions can change the state by committing mutations and can perform asynchronous operations.

Action declaration

Let's see how actions are declared inside a `Vuex` store:

```
const store = new Vuex.Store({
  state: {
    messages: [],
  },
  mutations: {
    addNewMessage(state, msgText) {
      state.messages.push({ text: msgText, read: false });
    },
  },
  actions: {
    addMessage(context, msgText) {
      API.addMessage(msgText).then(() => {
        context.commit('addNewMessage', msgText);
      });
    },
  },
});
```

In a similar way as that used for mutations, to declare an action, you write the action method inside the `actions` section of the `config` object provided to the `Vuex` store.

The action receives a `context` object and the action payload. The `context` object contains a `commit(...)` method and the `state` property, which is the application state.

In the preceding example, the `addMessage(...)` action sends the message text to a hypothetical server and, after the server response, it commits the corresponding mutation.

Dispatching an action

If you remember, Flux has a single dispatcher that dispatches actions to every store. It is the same in Vuex, except that there is only a single store, which is also a dispatcher. This means that actions can be dispatched using the store, as shown in the code below:

```
store.dispatch('addNewMessage', 'A message');
```

In the following code, I updated the `add message` example to use the `addMessage` action instead of directly using the `addNewMessage` mutation:

```
Vue.use(Vuex);

// Server API mock
const API = {
  addMessage: () => Promise.resolve()
};

const store = new Vuex.Store({
  state: {
    messages: [],
  },
  mutations: {
    addNewMessage(state, msgText) {
      state.messages.push({ text: msgText, read: false });
    },
  },
  actions: {
    addMessage(context, msgText) {
      API.addMessage(msgText).then(() => {
        context.commit('addNewMessage', msgText);
      });
    },
  },
});

const MessageList = {
  // ...
};

const MessageEditor = {
  template: `<div>
    <input type="text" v-model="message">
    <button @click="addMessage">Add message</button>
  </div>
  `,
  data() {
    return {
      message: '',
    };
  },
  methods: {
    addMessage() {
      this.$store.dispatch('addMessage', this.message);
    },
```

```
  },
};

new Vue({
  // ...
});
```

You are probably now thinking that there must be some helper to dispatch actions... in fact, there is!

The mapActions helper

Similar to the other helpers, the `mapActions` helper can be used inside the `methods` section of a `Vue` component. The syntax is the same as that of the other helpers:

```
const MessageEditor = {
  template: `<div>
    <input type="text" v-model="message">
    <button @click="addMessage(message)">
      Add message
    </button>
  </div>
  `,
  data() {
    return {
      message: '',
    };
  },
  methods: Vuex.mapActions(['addMessage']),
  // Or you can use the Object syntax
  // methods: Vuex.mapActions({ addMessage: 'addMessage' }),
};
```

Using modules for better scalability

Vuex's single state tree can be divided into modules. This is useful when the application grows larger and you want to split the app into groups of features. Doing so also lets you only load core features when the page loads, and allows you to load the other functionalities later. This way, you can reduce loading times drastically, especially if the connection is slow or the application is run inside a low-end mobile phone. It takes time for the JavaScript virtual machine to parse all the JavaScript code, thus providing only a single huge file with all the application code will take seconds to be parsed, giving a mobile user the impression that the application is slow and heavy.

A good tool to use in combination with Vue/Vuex is webpack, which lets you split your application into bundles. A webpack bundle can contain one or more Vuex modules, and a module can be loaded after another module. You can find more information about webpack at https://webpack.js.org/.

The application state tree can be split into modules, and each module into submodules. Let's see how this can be coded:

```
const subModule = {
  state: { ... },
  mutations: { ... },
  actions: { ... }
};

const moduleA = {
  state: { ... },
  mutations: { ... },
  actions: { ... },
  getters: { ... },
  modules: {
    sub: subModule
  }
};

const moduleB = {
  state: { ... },
  mutations: { ... },
  actions: { ... }
};

const store = new Vuex.Store({
  modules: {
    a: moduleA,
    b: moduleB
  }
});

store.state.a // -> `moduleA`'s state
store.state.a.sub // -> `subModule`'s state
store.state.b // -> `moduleB`'s state
```

As you can see, the object passed to new Vuex.store({}) is just the root module of your app, and inside the root module, or any other module, you can declare other modules.

Module local state

The state object passed to `mutations`, `actions`, and `getters` is the local module state. In this way, a submodule doesn't need to know it is inside another module.

But what if a submodule wants to access a parent module? The `rootState` is provided inside `actions` and `getters` so that you can navigate down to the desired module from the `rootState`. Let's see how:

```
const moduleA = {
  // ...
  actions: {
    incrementIfOddOnRootSum ({ state, commit, rootState }) {
      if ((state.count + rootState.count) % 2 === 1) {
        commit('increment');
      }
    }
  },
  getters: {
    sumWithRootCount (state, getters, rootState) {
      return state.count + rootState.count;
    }
  }
}
```

It is important to note that inside an action, the `rootState` is a property of the parameter `context` that is passed to the action, whereas inside a `getter`, the `rootState` is passed as the third parameter.

Module with namespace

There may be collisions between the names among different modules. To avoid this, and to create `reusable` modules, you can set the module's `namespaced` property to `true`. The following is an example of a `namespaced` module:

```
modules: {
  auth: {
    namespaced: true,
    state: { ... }, // Already nested, not affected by namespace
    mutations: {
      setLogged() {...} // -> commit('auth.setLogged')
    },
    actions: {
      login(){...} // -> dispatch('auth/login')
    },
```

```
  getters: {
    logged() {...} // -> getters['auth/logged']
  }
};
```

The code inside a module doesn't change when the `namespaced` property is set to `true`. What changes is the code that wants to use another `namespace` module. Look at the following example:

```
modules: {
  foo: {
    namespaced: true,
    getters: {
      someGetter (state, getters, rootState, rootGetters) {
        getters.someOtherGetter // -> 'foo/someOtherGetter'
        rootGetters.someOtherGetter // -> 'someOtherGetter'
      },
      someOtherGetter: state => { ... }
    },
    actions: {
      someAction ({dispatch, commit, getters, rootGetters}) {
        getters.someGetter // -> 'foo/someGetter'
        rootGetters.someGetter // -> 'someGetter'

        dispatch('someOtherAction'); //->'foo/someOtherAction'

        // -> 'someOtherAction'
        dispatch('someOtherAction', null, { root: true });

        commit('someMutation') // -> 'foo/someMutation'

        // -> 'someMutation'
        commit('someMutation', null, { root: true })
      },
      someOtherAction (ctx, payload) { ... }
    }
  }
}
```

To commit a mutation or dispatch an action of another module, you need to add `{ root: true }` as the third parameter. There is also a `rootGetters` parameter that is provided to the `actions` handlers or `getters` functions.

Finally, when using Vuex helpers, you need to specify the namespace as follows:

```
computed: {
  ...mapState('some/nested/module', {
    a: state => state.a,
    b: state => state.b
  })
},
methods: {
  ...mapActions('some/nested/module', [
    'foo',
    'bar'
  ])
}
```

Or you can create namespaced helpers using the function createNamespacedHelpers(nameSpace) which returns all the helpers inside an object. These helpers are bound to the namespace you provided as the first argument. The following is an example of how to use createNamespacedHelpers:

```
const { mapState, mapActions } =
    Vuex.createNamespacedHelpers('some/nested/module');

export default {
  computed: {
    // look up in `some/nested/module`
    ...mapState({
      a: state => state.a,
      b: state => state.b
    })
  },
  methods: {
    // look up in `some/nested/module`
    ...mapActions([
      'foo',
      'bar'
    ])
  }
};
```

At the end of this chapter, you will find an example of two modules with the namespace parameter set to true.

Dynamic module registration

It is possible to register a module after a Vuex store has been created using the `store.registerModule(...)` method. The following is an example of how a module can be registered:

```
// register a module `myModule`
store.registerModule('myModule', {
  // ...
})

// register a nested module `nested/myModule`
store.registerModule(['nested', 'myModule'], {
  // ...
})
```

This is particularly useful when modules are loaded asynchronously:

```
// Loading module asynchronously
// index.js
Vue.use(Vuex);

const store = new Vuex.Store({
  state: {
    currentView: 'initial'
  },
});

Vue.component('initial', {
  template: '<div>initial</div>',
});

import ('./loaded-later-moudle.js').then((module) => {
  module.default(store);
});

new Vue({
  el: '#app',
  template: '<component :is="$store.state.currentView"/>',
  store,
});
```

Following is `loaded-later-moudle.js` file code, which gets loaded inside `index.js`:

```
// loaded-later-moudle.js
export default function moduleFactory(store) {
  Vue.component('later', {
```

```
      template: '<div>later</div>',
    });

  store.registerModule('loadedLater', {});

  setTimeout(() => {
    store.state.currentView = 'later';
  }, 500);
}
```

In the preceding example, the root module defines a `currentView` property that points to the `initial` component. With the dynamic import syntax, we import the `loaded-later-moudle.js` file, and after it has been loaded we execute the module code that replaces the `currentView` value, causing the `later` component to be displayed.

The preceding example works inside a browser that supports dynamic import syntax, or you can use webpack to build it.

You can also unregister a dynamic loaded module by using `store.unregisterModule(moduleName)`. Static loaded modules cannot be unregistered.

Module reuse

As with Vue `components`, in order to reuse a module, the state declaration needs to be a function returning the state instead of a plain object. Otherwise, the state object is shared among all the module users. There are two cases where this may happen:

- Where multiple stores are using the same module
- Where the same module has been registered more than once in the same store

The first case is unlikely to happen because Vuex uses a single store. Besides, you can always create more than one store, even though you can register only one store per Vue instance.

The second case is likely to happen if the module is general purpose and depends on some parameters. In the same way that classes can have constructor parameters, a module could be created using a factory method with parameters. For example, say that you have two similar RESTful APIs and you created a generic API module so that the module can be used for both the APIs. In this case, you will use two instances of the same module, one for each API.

The following is an example of how to create a `reusable` module:

```
const ReusableModule = {
  state () {
    return {
      foo: 'bar'
    }
  },
  // mutations, actions, getters...
};
```

Enabling strict mode while developing

When `Vuex` is in strict mode, it will throw an error if the single state tree is mutated outside mutation handlers. This is useful when developing to prevent accidental modifications to the state. To enable strict mode, you just need to add `strict: true` to the store configuration object:

```
const store = new Vuex.Store({
  // ...
  strict: true
});
```

Strict mode should not be used in production. Strict mode runs a synchronous deep watcher on the state tree for detecting inappropriate mutations, and this can slow down the application. To avoid changing strict to `false` each time you want to create a production bundle, you should use a build tool that makes the strict value `false` when creating the production bundle. For example, you could use the following snippet in conjunction with webpack:

```
const store = new Vuex.Store({
  // ...
  strict: process.env.NODE_ENV !== 'production'
})
```

In `Chapter 3`, *Implementing Notes App Using Vuex State Management*, you will be shown how to use webpack to enable/disable strict mode.

Form handling restrictions when using Vuex

Using Vue's v-model feature with the Vuex state results in a direct modification of the state, which is forbidden.

Take a look at the following example:

```
<input v-model="$store.state.message">
```

In this example, $store.state is mutated directly by v-model, and if strict mode is enabled, it will result in an error being thrown.

There is more than one way to solve this problem, and I will show you the one that, in my opinion, is better: You can use a mutable computed property that accesses the state property when read and commits a mutation when set:

```
<input v-model="message">
// ...
computed: {
  message: {
    get () {
      return this.$store.state.obj.message;
    },
    set (value) {
      this.$store.commit('updateMessage', value);
    }
  }
}
```

Using a mutable computed property also allows you to add some validation before committing the corresponding mutation.

The following is a possible code for the mutation that gets committed:

```
// ...
mutations: {
  updateMessage (state, message) {
    state.obj.message = message;
  }
}
```

A simple counter example

The following is a very simple example of a counter that summarizes the core concepts of Vuex in a self-contained HTML file:

```html
<!DOCTYPE html>
<html lang="en">
<head>
  <meta charset="UTF-8">
  <title>Simple counter example</title>
</head>
<body>
<div id="app"></div>
<script src="https://unpkg.com/vuex@3.0.1/dist/vuex.min.js"></script>
<script src="https://unpkg.com/vue@2.5.13/dist/vue.min.js"></script>
<script>
  Vue.use(Vuex);

  // Sequential module
  const sequential = {
    namespaced: true,
    state() {
      return {
        count: 1,
      };
    },
    mutations: {
      increment: state => state.count++,
      decrement: state => state.count--
    },
    actions: {
      increment: ({ commit }) => commit('increment'),
      decrement: ({ commit }) => commit('decrement'),
    },
    getters: {
      name: () => 'Sequential',
      currentCount: state => state.count,
    },
  };

  // FizzBuzz module that extends sequential module
  // and redefine some functions.
  const fizzBuzz = Object.assign({}, sequential, {
    getters: {
      name: () => 'FizzBuzz',
      currentCount: state => {
        const { count } = state;
```

```
        let msg = '';
        if (count % 3 === 0) msg += "Fizz";
        if (count % 5 === 0) msg += "Buzz";
        return `${count} ${msg}`;
      },
    },
  });

  // Application store with the two modules
  const store = new Vuex.Store({
    modules: {
      sequential,
      fizzBuzz,
    },
  });

  // HTML template to show the result
  const template = `
  <div>
    <button @click="increment">+</button>
    <button @click="decrement">-</button>
    <span>{{name}} value: {{currentCount}}</span>
  </div>
`;

  // counter component
  const counter = {
    template,
    computed: Vuex.mapGetters('sequential', [
      'name',
      'currentCount',
    ]),
    methods: Vuex.mapActions('sequential', [
      'increment',
      'decrement',
    ]),
  };

  // fizzBuzzCounter component
  const fizzBuzzCounter = {
    template,
    computed: Vuex.mapGetters('fizzBuzz', [
      'name',
      'currentCount',
    ]),
    methods: Vuex.mapActions('fizzBuzz', [
      'increment',
      'decrement',
```

```
   ]),
 };

 // Vue instance with the store and the components
 new Vue({
   el: '#app',
   store,
   template: '<div><counter></counter>' +
   '<fizzBuzzCounter></fizzBuzzCounter></div>',
   components: {
     counter,
     fizzBuzzCounter,
   },
 });
</script>
</body>
</html>
```

The preceding example shows two counters. The first one just increments or decrements the current value. The second one, **FizzBuzz**, shows *Fizz* if the counter is divisible by 3, *Buzz* if it is divisible by 5, and **FizzBuzz** when it is both divisible by 3 and 5, as shown in the following screenshot:

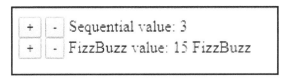

Figure 2.2: FizzBuzz counter

In this example, I created two modules and two components that use these modules: one for the `sequential` counter and the other for the `fizzBuzz` counter.

After that, I created a new instance of `Vue` and added the two modules and components to it. The aim of this example is to show you how to use `namespaced` modules, as well as to serve as a full but simple example of Vue and Vuex combined together.

You can find the example source code inside the GitHub repository of this book in the `chapter-2/fizzbuzz-counter` folder .

Summary

In this chapter, we studied the Vuex framework. We went through its core concepts and saw how Vuex can be integrated into a Vue application. At the end, a simple counter example helped us to get the whole picture.

It is now time to move from a simple example to real application development using Vuex. That is the topic of `Chapter 3`, *Implementing the Notes App Using Vuex State Management*, developing an application that takes notes in a similar way to Google Keep or Evernote.

Setting Up Development and Test Environment

3

When I started using Vue, I found it difficult to integrate Vue with webpack. I also had trouble configuring Karma to use webpack for my tests, not to mention figuring out how to test single file components!

For this reason, in the next pages you will be guided through the process of configuring an environment ready for both Vue/Vuex development and testing. I think you will find the next pages quite useful.

In this chapter you will:

- set up the development environment using npm.
- install, configure and use webpack.
- install, configure and use vue-loader.
- set up the testing environment using Karma + Jasmine.

Technical requirements

You will be required to have Node.js installed on a system. Finally, to use the Git repository of this book, the user needs to install Git.

The code files of this chapter can be found on GitHub:
`https://github.com/PacktPublishing/Vuex-Quick-Start-Guide/tree/master/chapter-3`

Check out the following video to see the code in action:
`https://goo.gl/oacFdP`

Setting up the development environment

Vue provides a tool, vue-cli, for scaffolding Vue.js projects. It also supports webpack, the web packaging tool we are going to use. To install vue-cli, you just need to type npm install -g vue-cli in a console.

Although using vue-cli is the fastest way to start a new project, in the following paragraphs, I will explain how to set up a Vue project from scratch.

We will set up a Vue/Vuex project using the **npm** (**node package manager**), explaining every step and installing only a minimum set of dependencies, as opposed to vue-cli, which will install a lot of npm packages in order to provide a general-purpose project configuration.

By using the GitHub repository of this book and checking out the first commits, you can observe what I did to set up the *EveryNote* app development environment.

Using npm to prepare the project for Vue/Vuex

To use npm, you need to have Node.js installed. You can find information on how to install Node.js at https://nodejs.org/.

The first step to make a Vue/Vuex project is creating a directory and initializing it with npm. Open a console and type the following commands:

```
mkdir notes-app
cd notes-app
npm init
```

The npm init command will ask you some questions. Each question has a default value that is normally a good choice. You can just press *Enter* for each question. After that, it will create a package.json file with the values you provided. We will use this file to save project dependencies and to create some commands that are useful for the app's development.

Let's begin by installing webpack and its related utilities. Webpack is a module bundler, and it will help us to create the production bundles, as well as handle Vue single-file components. If you have never used webpack, you should google it to familiarize yourself with its core principles. From now on, I will assume that you have basic knowledge of webpack. Type the following commands in the console:

```
npm install --save-dev webpack
npm install --save-dev webpack-cli
npm install --save-dev webpack-dev-server
npm install --save-dev html-webpack-plugin
npm install --save-dev clean-webpack-plugin
```

A directory named `node_modules` has been created, and you can find the source code of the packages we have just installed inside this directory. If you use `Git`, `node_modules` should be put inside `.gitignore`. The `--save-dev` option writes the five package names we've just installed to the `package.json` file. This way, each time you type `npm install`, all saved packages will be downloaded, if needed.

Let's see what these packages do:

- `webpack`: Will take all the source files and bundle them into a folder that will have the corresponding production files
- `webpack-dev-server`: Starts a development HTTP server, and helps us to write code and debug it in the browser
- `html-webpack-plugin`: Will help us create an `index.html` that will load the webpack bundle file
- `clean-webpack-plugin`: Removes the distribution folder created by webpack when bundling the project

By typing `npm install`, all the saved packages will be reinstalled inside the `node_modules` folder. This way, to initialize a project, you just need to get the code (using `git clone`, for example) and type `npm install`, and the project will be ready to be used.

Let's now create a file named `webpack.config.js` to configure webpack. The initial file will look like the following:

```
// webpack.config.js
const path = require('path');
const HtmlWebpackPlugin = require('html-webpack-plugin');
const CleanWebpackPlugin = require('clean-webpack-plugin');
const webpack = require('webpack');
```

```
const config = {
  entry: {
    app: './src/main.js',
  },
  output: {
    filename: '[name].bundle.js',
    path: path.resolve(__dirname, 'dist/'),
  },
  plugins: [
    new HtmlWebpackPlugin({ template: 'src/index.html' }),
    new CleanWebpackPlugin(['dist']),
    new webpack.DefinePlugin({
      'process.env.NODE_ENV': JSON.stringify(process.env.NODE_ENV ||
'development'),
    }),
  ]
};

module.exports = config;
```

In the preceding configuration, we assumed that we have a folder named `src`, and inside we have an `index.html` and a `main.js`.

You may also have noticed that I used `webpack.DefinePlugin`: This plugin lets you define constants that can be used inside the project. In this case, we define `process.env.NODE_ENV` to tell the development environment apart from the production one.

Now we can create the `src` folder:

mkdir src

Once this is done, create the `index.html` file inside the `src` folder:

```
<!-- src/index.html -->
<!DOCTYPE html>
<html lang="en">
<head>
  <meta charset="UTF-8">
  <title>Packt: Vuex condensed</title>
</head>
<body>
Hello world
</body>
</html>
```

Now write the `main.js` file, as follows:

```
// src/main.js
console.log('Hello world');
```

We can now use webpack to build the project. We can use the `npx` node command, which executes npm package binaries, saving us from having to write the whole path to the webpack executable:

npx webpack --config webpack.config.js

A folder named `dist` will be created, and inside you will find the `app.bundle.js` and `index.html` files. If you open the HTML file, you may notice that the following line has been added at the end of the body tag:

```
<script type="text/javascript" src="app.bundle.js"></script>
```

That is the `html` tag that will load the webpack bundle. We will see later how to tell webpack to use Vue single-file components.

Since building each individual bundle and loading them in an HTTP server to see the changes during development is not convenient, we will use `webpack-dev-server`:

npx webpack-dev-server --config webpack.config.js

If you open a browser at `http://localhost:8080/`, you will see a white page with a **Hello world** phrase inside. If you open the browser development tools, you will see the same sentence printed in the browser console.

Let's put some commands to run webpack and `webpack-dev-server` inside the `package.json` file so that we can run them by typing `npm run build` and `npm start`:

```
{
  "name": "notes-app",
  "version": "1.0.0",
  ...
  "scripts": {
    "start": "webpack-dev-server --mode development",
    "build": "cross-env NODE_ENV=production webpack --mode production"
  },
  ...
  "devDependencies": {
    "clean-webpack-plugin": "^0.1.17",
    "html-webpack-plugin": "^2.30.1",
    "webpack": "^3.10.0",
```

```
    "webpack-dev-server": "^2.11.0"
  }
}
```

Since webpack 4.0, you have needed to specify whether you are running webpack for a production environment or a development one. The `--mode` parameter lets you specify which environment you are building for. Finally, `--config webpack.config.js` can be omitted.

You may have noticed that I added `cross-env NODE_ENV=production` in the `build` section. That's because, when building the application for production, we need the `NODE_ENV` environment variable to be set to a production value. This way, we can use something like the following code to determine whether we are building production code:

```
const debug = process.env.NODE_ENV !== 'production';
```

To use `cross-env`, you need to install it by typing:

npm install --save-dev cross-env

Finally, let's install Vue and Vuex and use them to check whether everything is properly configured.

Execute the following command in a console:

npm install --save vue vuex

Edit the `main.js` file as follows:

```
import Vue from 'vue';
import Vuex from 'vuex';

Vue.use(Vuex);
const store = new Vuex.Store({});
new Vue({
  el: '#app',
  store,
  template:'<div>Hello Vue(x) World!</div>'
});
```

Update `index.html` as follows:

```
<!DOCTYPE html>
<html lang="en">
<head>
  <meta charset="UTF-8">
  <title>Packt: Vuex condensed</title>
```

```
    </head>
    <body>
    <div id="app"></div>
    </body>
    </html>
```

Now type `npm start` and voila—the browser shows our very first Vuex application: `Hello Vue(x) World!`

Using vue-loader for single-file components

Vue.js provides a webpack loader, `vue-loader`, to transform single-file components into JavaScript modules. To install `vue-loader` and related tools, type the following commands into a console:

```
npm install --save-dev vue-loader
npm install --save-dev vue-template-compiler
npm install --save-dev vue-style-loader
npm install --save-dev css-loader
npm install --save-dev file-loader
```

The `file-loader` is needed to import external files, such as images. The other packages are needed to tell webpack how to build all the pieces inside the `.vue` file.

Let's update `webpack.config.js` to use single-file components that will have a file extension of `.vue`:

```
// ...
const config = {
  // ...
  module: {
    rules: [
      {
        test: /\.vue$/,
        loader: 'vue-loader'
      },
      {
        test: /\.css$/,
        use: [
          'vue-style-loader',
          'css-loader'
        ]
      },
      {
        test: /\.(png|jpg|jpeg|gif|svg)$/,
```

```
      loader: 'file-loader',
      options: {
        name: '[name].[ext]?[hash]'
      }
    }
  ]
},
resolve: {
  alias: {
    vue$: 'vue/dist/vue.esm.js',
  },
},
// ...
};
// ...
```

Within the `rules` section inside the configuration, we tell webpack which loader to use when a file is imported inside a source file. In the preceding code, we configured webpack to use `vue-loader` for every `.vue` file, `css-loader`, and `vue-style-loader` for `.css` files, and `file-loader` for images.

In order to test that everything has been correctly configured, we will create an `app.vue` file:

```
// src/app.vue
<template>
  <div class="app">App <span class="version">v{{version}}</span></div>
</template>
<script>
  export default {
    computed: {
      version() {
        return this.$store.state.version;
      }
    }
  };
</script>
<style>
  .app {
    font-family: "Times New Roman", Times, serif;
    background-image: url("./background.jpg");
  }
</style>
```

You need a `background.jpg` file to build the preceding file. It is enough to put any image within the `src` folder and rename it as `background.jpg`.

This file uses `Vuex.Store`, the three parts of a Vue single-file
component—`<template>`, `<script>`, and `<style>`—and an image as the background.
This way, we are going to test `vue-loader` and its related packages, `Vuex.Store`,
and `file-loader` for the background image.

Let's now update `main.js` to use `app.vue`:

```
// src/main.js
import Vue from 'vue';
import Vuex from 'vuex';
import app from './app.vue';

Vue.use(Vuex);

const store = new Vuex.Store({
  state: {
    version: '1.0.0'
  }
});

new Vue({
  el: '#app',
  store,
  template:'<app></app>',
  components: {app}
});
```

Restart `webpack-dev-server` (`npm start`) and open the
URL `http://localhost:8080/`, and you will see something like the following screenshot:

Figure 3.1: Using app.vue

Configuring the test environment

If you are configuring webpack for single-file components, you will probably find it a bit tricky; configuring a test environment is definitely difficult the first time.

We will use Karma as the test runner, Jasmine as the test/assertions framework, and Chrome as the browser that will run all the tests.

First, let's install all we need:

```
npm install --save-dev karma karma-webpack
npm install --save-dev karma-chrome-launcher
npm install --save-dev jasmine-core karma-jasmine
```

Then we need to create a `karma.conf.js` file, as follows:

```
// Using webpack configuration
var webpackConfig = require('./webpack.config.js');
delete webpackConfig.entry; // No entry for tests

module.exports = function(config) {
  config.set({
    basePath: '',
    frameworks: ['jasmine'],
    files: [
      'test/**/*.spec.js'
    ],
    exclude: [
    ],
    preprocessors: {
      'test/**/*.spec.js': ['webpack']
    },
    reporters: ['progress'],
    port: 9876,
    colors: true,
    logLevel: config.LOG_INFO,
    autoWatch: true,
    browsers: ['Chrome'],
    singleRun: false,
    concurrency: Infinity,
    webpack: webpackConfig,

    // avoid walls of useless text
    webpackMiddleware: {
      noInfo: true
    }
  })
```

```
};
```

The preceding configuration will run all files that end with .spec.js inside the test folder. In addition, we told Karma to preprocess files using webpack.

Let's create a test folder inside notes-app:

```
mkdir test
```

Finally, we will create a simple test that will load a .vue file and test it.

Create a folder inside test named test-setup and put it inside a dummy.vue file:

```
// test/test-setup/dummy.vue
<template>
  <div class="app">{{msg}}</div>
</template>
<script>
  export default {
    data() {
      return {msg: 'A message'};
    }
  };
</script>
```

Create a test file named dummy.vue.spec.js:

```
// test/test-setup/dummy.vue.spec.js
import Vue from 'vue';
import Test from './dummy.vue';

describe('dummy.vue', function () {
  it('should have correct message', function () {
    expect(Test.data().msg).toBe('A message');
  });

  it('should render correct message', function () {
    const vm = new Vue({
      template: '<div><test></test></div>',
      components: {
        'test': Test
      }
    }).$mount();
    expect(vm.$el.querySelector('.app').textContent)
      .toBe('A message');
  })
});
```

Update `package.json` as follows:

```
"scripts": {
    "test": "karma start",
    "start": "webpack-dev-server --config webpack.config.js",
    "build": "webpack --config webpack.config.js"
},
```

Next, execute `npm test` to run the test we just created. You should see something like the following in the console:

```
Chrome ... : Executed 2 of 2 SUCCESS (0.006 secs / 0 secs)
```

We are now ready to begin the development of the EveryNote web application, which is the topic of the next chapter.

Summary

In this chapter we went through all the steps necessary to set up a test and development environment, ready to start coding with Vuex and Vue single file components. In addition we added some files to test that everything was properly configured.

4
Coding the EveryNote App Using Vuex State Management

In this chapter, we will develop an application to take notes, called *EveryNote*, from scratch. In the first part of the chapter we will analyze and design the application, as well as preparing the folder structure for the project.

After that, we will build the application incrementally through tests and code. This application will be developed while writing this chapter, providing a real-world Vuex development example.

The application can be downloaded by cloning the `https://github.com/PacktPublishing/-Vuex-Condensed` Git repository. Each section of this chapter has a corresponding Git tag that can be used to download the code that has been written for that section.

While reading this chapter, you will learn how to do the following:

- Design and develop an application exploiting Vuex features
- Use Vuex inside Vue components
- Test Vue/Vuex components effectively
- Use actions to handle asynchronous operations

Technical requirements

You will be required to have Node.js installed on a system. Finally, to use the Git repository of this book, the user needs to install Git.

The code files of this chapter can be found on GitHub:
`https://github.com/PacktPublishing/Vuex-Quick-Start-Guide/tree/master/chapter-4`

Check out the following video to see the code in action:
`https://goo.gl/QaPP1Q`

Designing the EveryNote web app

One way to start designing an application is by creating mock-ups of the user interfaces. This way, you can present your mock-ups to your stakeholders, discuss them, update your mock-ups accordingly, and resubmit them to stakeholders. This can be done before you start developing.

The **EveryNote** app will look like the following mock-up:

Figure 3.2: EveryNote mock-up interface

The application will have the following features:

- Create new notes
- Show all notes
- Update an existing note
- Delete a note
- Save notes to `LocalStorage`

After basic features are implemented, we will also add two more features:

- Search among notes
- Pin a note

In a real-world application, you may need user stories to better define what the behaviors expected are and, thus, what programmers should code. These stories can be tested, and this type of test is called an acceptance test.

In this case, the EveryNote features are simple and well defined, so we can begin by picking a feature and starting to develop it.

Application structure

Vuex proposes an application-generic structure, which we will adopt. The following is the folder structure:

```
test # test folder
├── test_file.spec.js # a test file
└── ...
src # app main folder
├── index.html
├── main.js
├── api
│   └── ... # abstractions for making API requests
├── components
│   ├── App.vue
│   └── ...
└── store
    ├──index.js #here we assemble modules and export the store
    ├── actions.js # root actions
    ├── mutations.js # root mutations
    └── modules
        ├── module_a.js # a module
        └── module_b.js # another module
```

We are now going to create the project scaffold by adding some files to the `notes-app` folder we created at the beginning of this chapter.

The first file to be created is `index.html`. As for any Vue.js application, we need to put the root container for the Vue/Vuex application inside the body as follows:

```
<!-- src/index.html -->
<!DOCTYPE html>
```

```
<html lang="en">
<head>
  <meta charset="UTF-8">
  <title>Packt: Vuex condensed EveryNote</title>
</head>
<body>
<div id="app"></div>
</body>
</html>
```

The second file is `main.js`. It contains the code to startup the Vue.js part of the application:

```
// src/main.js
import Vue from 'vue';
import App from './components/App.vue';
import store from './store';

new Vue({
  el: '#app',
  store,
  render: h => h(App),
});
```

Now that the Vue application is ready, we can add Vuex to it by creating `index.js` inside the `store` folder:

```
// src/store/index.js
import Vuex from 'vuex';
import Vue from 'vue';

Vue.use(Vuex);

const debug = process.env.NODE_ENV !== 'production';
const store = new Vuex.Store({
 state: {},
 strict: debug,
});

export default store;
```

Finally, we create the root Vue component of the *EveryNote* app as follows:

```
// src/components/App.vue
<template>
 <div class="app">EveryNote app</div>
</template>
<script>
 export default {};
```

```
</script>
<style>
 .app {
 font-family: "Times New Roman", Times, serif;
 background-image: url("background.jpeg");
 }
</style>
```

Clone the `book` repository and use `git checkout step-0_project-scaffold` to see all the project files for this step.

Now that the project scaffold is ready, we can start coding the first feature.

Developing the EveryNote app

In the following paragraphs, I will develop the application using test-driven development. You don't need to know TDD to understand what I will be doing. You will first be presented with a test asserting what the code should do as if it were already implemented, and then, just after, you will see the implementation.

But why use TDD in this book?

One reason is that I think it is easier to understand what the code is supposed to do by reading assertions about its behavior inside the test code, rather than inferring its behavior from implementation code.

Another reason is that it is easier to understand how to test a component while writing the component rather than having a (boring) chapter on testing components.

Using a to-do list to help the development process

I find that writing a to-do list in a file is useful for reminding me what needs to be done. I also find it helpful to note down doubts and simple notes on things I need to deal with.

This to-do list is a simple `.txt` file that changes over time, and will hopefully be empty when the app is finished. I also put this file under `Git revision`.

The initial `To-do` list looks like this:

```
To-do:
Show all notes*
Create new notes
Update an existing note
Delete a note
Save notes to LocalStorage

Extra:
Search among notes
Pin a note

Done:
```

I use the * symbol to mark the current feature under development.

Displaying a list of notes

I will start by displaying a list of notes because the other features depend on it. Another possible feature to start with is the ability to create a new note.

In order to display a list of notes, we need to add that list to the application's `Vuex.Store`. Then we need a Vue component that uses the store to display the notes.

The first test is about defining a note list inside the application's main store:

```
// test/store/store.spec.js
import store from '../../src/store';

describe('EveryNote main store', () => {
  it('should have a list of notes', () => {
    expect(Array.isArray(store.state.noteList)).toBe(true);
  });
});
```

Next, define the implementation:

```
// src/store/index.js

import ...
// ...
const store = new Vuex.Store({
  state: {
    noteList: [],
  },
```

```
    strict: debug,
  });
  ...
```

From now on, you will first see a frame detailing a component's tests, and, just after, a frame with the code implementation. You will be provided with a description of test-driven development later on in this chapter. For now, it is important that you understand that TDD has a pace: one test, one piece of production code, one test, one piece of production code, and so on.

This is also referred to as red, green, refactor:

- **Red**: You write a small test and the result of executing it is a test failing—you'll see red in the test console.
- **Green**: You make the test pass in the easiest way—you'll see green in the test console. Duplicating code in this step is allowed.
- **Refactor**: You remove code duplication and improve code quality if you feel it is necessary.

The next step is creating a Vue component `noteList` to show the list of notes.

Test code:

```
// test/components/NoteList.spec.js
import Vue from 'vue';
import Vuex from 'vuex';
import NoteList from '../../src/components/NoteList.vue';

describe('NoteList.vue', () => {
  let store;
  let noteList;

  function newNoteListCmp() {
    const Constructor = Vue.extend(NoteList);
    return new Constructor({
      store,
    }).$mount();
  }

  beforeEach(() => {
    Vue.use(Vuex);

    noteList = [];
    store = new Vuex.Store({
      state: { noteList },
    });
```

```
  });

  it('should expose store.noteList', () => {
    const noteListCmp = newNoteListCmp();

    expect(noteListCmp.notes).toBe(noteList);
  });

  it('should cycle through noteList', () => {
    noteList.push({});
    noteList.push({});

    const noteListCmp = newNoteListCmp();

    const contents =
      noteListCmp.$el.querySelectorAll('.content');
    expect(contents.length).toBe(2);
  });

  it('should render notes inside noteList', () => {
    const title = 'Note title';
    const content = 'Note content';
    noteList.push({ title, content });

    const noteListCmp = newNoteListCmp();

    const { $el } = noteListCmp;
    const titleEl = $el.querySelector('.title');
    const contentEl = $el.querySelector('.content');
    expect(titleEl.textContent).toBe(title);
    expect(contentEl.textContent).toBe(content);
  });
});
```

Application code:

```
// src/components/NoteList.vue
<template>
  <div class="container">
    <div v-for="note in notes">
      <div class="title">{{note.title}}</div>
      <div class="content">{{note.content}}</div>
    </div>
  </div>
</template>
<script>
  import { mapState } from 'vuex';
```

```
export default {
  computed: mapState({
    notes: 'noteList',
  }),
};
</script>
<style>
</style>
```

Even though I put together all of these tests in one place for better readability, I didn't write the three tests and then the code. I wrote the first test, then the code, then the next test, and so on. Remember the red-green-refactor pattern!

In order to write the `NoteList` code I needed three tests:

- The first test checks that there is a computed property named `notes` that exposes `state.store.NoteList`
- The second test ensures that each note inside `notes` is rendered in the template section
- Finally, the last test ensures that the note's title and content are rendered

In addition, there is some code to set up the test environment in order to mock the store and create the component. Each item being tested should be isolated. This means that we cannot use the real store, and we need to provide a mocked one for each component being tested.

There is a framework, `vue-test-utils`, that can be used to test Vue components. I decided not to use it for the sake of keeping the examples in this book simple. You may want to use it when writing your applications.

We can now proceed to the next feature, but I would first like to see some notes actually shown in the browser before moving on. To achieve this, we can temporarily add two notes to the store and add the `NoteList` component to `App.vue`.

Test code:

```
// src/store/index.js
import Vuex from 'vuex';
import Vue from 'vue';

Vue.use(Vuex);

const debug = process.env.NODE_ENV !== 'production';
const store = new Vuex.Store({
  state: {
    noteList: [
```

```
      { title: 'title A', content: 'content 1' },
      { title: 'title B', content: 'content 2' },
    ],
  },
  strict: debug,
});

export default store;
```

Application code:

```
// src/components/App.vue
<template>
  <div class="app">
    <div>EveryNote app</div>
    <note-list></note-list>
  </div>
</template>
<script>
  import NoteList from './NoteList.vue';

  export default {
    components: {
      NoteList,
    },
  };
</script>
<style>
  .app {
    font-family: "Times New Roman", Times, serif;
    background-image: url("background.jpeg");
  }
</style>
```

The following is a screenshot of the result:

Figure 3.3: List of notes

Right now, the result is ugly; I will add some CSS to make it much better looking after all the main features are implemented.

You can download the code at this stage by typing:

```
git checkout step-1_note-list
```

Creating new notes

At this point, the To-do list looks like this:

```
To-do:
Create new notes*
- NoteEditor component
- Update current note mutation
- Add note to noteList mutation
- Add note action

Update an existing note
Delete a note
Save notes to LocalStorage

Extra:
Search among notes
Pin a note

Done:
Show all notes
  - Add note list to the store
  - Note list vue component
  -- Add a temporary note list to the store
```

The next feature I will implement is the ability to create new notes. For this feature, we need a NoteEditor component, a store property named currentNote, an action named addNote, and two mutations: UPDATE_CURRENT_NOTE and ADD_NOTE.

The idea is that when a user writes in the note editor, the currentNote store property gets updated. When he taps on the **Add note** button, the addNote action is fired, resulting in the new note added to the note list. Let's add the currentNote property to the application store.

Test code:

```
// test/store/store.spec.js
import store from '../../src/store';

describe('EveryNote main store', () => {
  it('should have a list of notes', () => {
    expect(Array.isArray(store.state.noteList)).toBe(true);
  });

  it('should have currentNote property', () => {
    const { state } = store;
    expect(state.currentNote.title).not.toBe(undefined);
    expect(state.currentNote.content).not.toBe(undefined);
  });
});
```

Application code:

```
// src/store/index.js

//...

const store = new Vuex.Store({
  state: {
    noteList: [
      { title: 'title A', content: 'content 1' },
      { title: 'title B', content: 'content 2' },
    ],
    currentNote: { title: '', content: '' },
  },
  mutations,
  strict: debug,
});
```

You may wonder why I added a test just to verify that the `currentNote` field is inside the app store. The idea here is that I am not writing tests to test that the application works properly—I am writing tests to write production code. In order to modify any line of the application code, I need a test to justify the fact that I am writing production code.

This is the first of the three TDD rules (by Robert C. Martin, aka Uncle Bob):

- You are not allowed to write any production code unless it makes a failing unit test pass

The other two are as follows:

- You are not allowed to write any more of a unit test that is sufficient to fail, and compilation failures are failures
- You are not allowed to write any more production code that is sufficient to pass the one failing unit test

So why didn't I write any tests when I added two fake notes to the store and modified `App.vue` to use the `NoteList` component? Because that is temporary code and not production code. I will remove those modifications before the app is completed.

Now that `currentNote` is defined, I can write an `UPDATE_CURRENT_NOTE` mutation.

Test code:

```
// test/store/mutations.spec.js
import { mutations, types } from '../../src/store/mutations';

describe('EveryNote root mutations', () => {
  it('should update current note', () => {
    const updateCurrentNote
      = mutations[types.UPDATE_CURRENT_NOTE];
    const state = { currentNote: { title: '', content: '' } };
    const newNote = { title: 'title', content: 'some text' };

    updateCurrentNote(state, newNote);

    expect(state.currentNote).toEqual(newNote);
  });
});
```

Application code:

```
// src/store/mutations.js
export const types = {
  UPDATE_CURRENT_NOTE: 'UPDATE_CURRENT_NOTE',
};

export const mutations = {
  [types.UPDATE_CURRENT_NOTE](state, { title, content }) {
    state.currentNote = { title, content };
  },
};
```

Next, create the `NoteEditor` component.

Test code:

```
// test/components/NoteEditor.spec.js
import Vue from 'vue';
import Vuex from 'vuex';
import NoteEditor from '../../src/components/NoteEditor.vue';
import { types, mutations } from '../../src/store/mutations';
import actions from '../../src/store/actions';

const { UPDATE_CURRENT_NOTE } = types;
describe('NoteEditor component', () => {
  let store;
  let currentNote;

  function newNoteEditorCmp() {
    const Constructor = Vue.extend(NoteEditor);
    store = new Vuex.Store({
            state: { currentNote, noteList: [] },
      mutations,
      actions,
    });
    return new Constructor({
      store,
    }).$mount();
  }

  beforeEach(() => {
    Vue.use(Vuex);
    currentNote = { title: 'title', content: 'content' };
  });

  it('should expose currentNote.content as content', () => {
    const editorCmp = newNoteEditorCmp();

    expect(editorCmp.content).toBe(currentNote.content);
  });

  it('should expose currentNote.content setter', () => {
    const editorCmp = newNoteEditorCmp();
    store.commit = jasmine.createSpy('commit spy');
    const newContent = 'A new content';

    editorCmp.content = newContent;

    const expected = {
```

```
      title: currentNote.title,
      content: newContent,
    };
    expect(store.commit)
      .toHaveBeenCalledWith(UPDATE_CURRENT_NOTE, expected);
  });

  it('should expose currentNote.title as title', () => {
    const editorCmp = newNoteEditorCmp();

    expect(editorCmp.title).toBe(currentNote.title);
  });

  it('should expose currentNote.title setter', () => {
    const editorCmp = newNoteEditorCmp();
    store.commit = jasmine.createSpy('commit spy');
    const newTitle = 'A new title';

    editorCmp.title = newTitle;

    const expected = {
      title: newTitle,
      content: currentNote.content,
    };
    expect(store.commit)
      .toHaveBeenCalledWith(UPDATE_CURRENT_NOTE, expected);
  });

  it('should render current note inside the editor', () => {
    const editorCmp = newNoteEditorCmp();

    const { $el } = editorCmp;
    const contentEl = $el.querySelector('.content');
    const titleEl = $el.querySelector('.title');
    expect(contentEl.value).toBe(currentNote.content);
    expect(titleEl.value).toBe(currentNote.title);
  });
});
```

Application code:

```
// src/components/NoteEditor.vue
<template>
  <div>
    <input v-model="title" type="text" class="title"/>
    <input v-model="content" type="text" class="content"/>
  </div>
</template>
```

```
<script>
  import { types } from '../store/mutations';

  const { UPDATE_CURRENT_NOTE } = types;
  export default {
    computed: {
      content: {
        get() {
          return this.$store.state.currentNote.content;
        },
        set(value) {
          const newContent = {
            title: this.title,
            content: value,
          };
          this.$store.commit(UPDATE_CURRENT_NOTE, newContent);
        },
      },
      title: {
        get() {
          return this.$store.state.currentNote.title;
        },
        set(value) {
          const newContent = {
            title: value,
            content: this.content,
          };
          this.$store.commit(UPDATE_CURRENT_NOTE, newContent);
        },
      },
    },
  };
</script>
<style></style>
```

In order to code the `NoteEditor` component, I tested that the computed `content` and `title` properties were properly linked to `$store.state.currentNote`, and that these properties were used in the `template` section.

As with the tests for the `NoteList` component, the first part of the `test` file is just some code to create the component under `test`. I will avoid repeating that part from now on.

The next step is creating the `addNote` action and the corresponding mutation so that I can update `NoteEditor` to dispatch this action when a user presses the **Add note** button. Following is the `ADD_NOTE` mutation.

Test code:

```
// test/store/mutations.spec.js
import { mutations, types } from '../../src/store/mutations';

describe('EveryNote root mutations', () => {
  it('should update current note', () => {
    // ...
  });

  it('should add a note to noteList', () => {
    const ADD_NOTE = mutations[types.ADD_NOTE];
    const state = { noteList: [] };
    const newNote = { title: 'title', content: 'some text' };

    ADD_NOTE(state, newNote);

    expect(state.noteList['0']).toBe(newNote);
  });
});
```

Application code:

```
// src/store/mutations.js
export const types = {
  UPDATE_CURRENT_NOTE: 'UPDATE_CURRENT_NOTE',
  ADD_NOTE: 'ADD_NOTE',
};

export const mutations = {
  [types.UPDATE_CURRENT_NOTE](state, { title, content }) {
    state.currentNote = { title, content };
  },
  [types.ADD_NOTE](state, aNote) {
    state.noteList.push(aNote);
  },
};
```

Following is the addNote action tests:

```
// test/store/actions.spec.js

import actions from '../../src/store/actions';
import { types } from '../../src/store/mutations';

describe('EveryNote root actions', () => {
  it('should have addNote action', () => {
    const { addNote } = actions;
```

```
    const mockContext = {
      commit: jasmine.createSpy('commit'),
    };
    const aNote = {};

    addNote(mockContext, aNote);

    expect(mockContext.commit)
      .toHaveBeenCalledWith(types.ADD_NOTE, aNote);
  });
});
```

Following is the application code:

```
// src/store/actions
import { types } from './mutations';

export default {
  addNote({ commit }, aNote) {
    commit(types.ADD_NOTE, aNote);
  },
};
```

Finally, I can update `NoteEditor` to dispatch the `addNote` action and see that the note list gets updated. First, let's update `NoteEditor`.

Test code:

```
// test/components/NoteEditor.spec.js
import // ...

const { UPDATE_CURRENT_NOTE } = types;
describe('NoteEditor component', () => {
  let store;
  let currentNote;

  function newNoteEditorCmp() {
    // ...
  }

  // ...

  it('should have addNote method', () => {
    const editorCmp = newNoteEditorCmp();
    spyOn(store, 'dispatch');

    editorCmp.addNote();
```

```
    expect(store.dispatch)
      .toHaveBeenCalledWith('addNote', currentNote);
  });

  it('should not add empty notes', () => {
    const editorCmp = newNoteEditorCmp();
    spyOn(store, 'dispatch');
    currentNote.title = '';
    currentNote.content = '';

    editorCmp.addNote();

    expect(store.dispatch).not.toHaveBeenCalled();
  });

  it('should reset title and content on addNote', () => {
    const editorCmp = newNoteEditorCmp();

    editorCmp.addNote();

    expect(editorCmp.title).toBe('');
    expect(editorCmp.content).toBe('');
  });
});
```

Application code:

```
// src/components/NoteEditor.vue
<template>
  <div>
    <input v-model="title" type="text" class="title"
           placeholder="title"/>
    <input v-model="content" type="text" class="content"
           placeholder="content"/>
    <button @click="addNote">Add note</button>
  </div>
</template>
<script>
  import { types } from '../store/mutations';

  const { UPDATE_CURRENT_NOTE } = types;
  export default {
    computed: {
      content: {
        // ...
      },
      title: {
        // ...
```

```
        },
      },
    methods: {
      addNote() {
        if (this.title !== '' || this.content !== '') {
          const newNote = {
            title: this.title,
            content: this.content,
          };

          this.$store.dispatch('addNote', newNote);
        }
        this.title = '';
        this.content = '';
      },
    },
  };
</script>
```

Now let's add actions to the store:

```
// src/store/index.js
import // ...
import actions from './actions';

// ...

const store = new Vuex.Store({
  state: { // ... },
  mutations,
  actions,
  strict: debug,
});
```

and NoteEditor to App.vue

```
// src/components/App.vue
<template>
  <div class="app">
    <div>EveryNote app</div>
    <note-editor></note-editor>
    <note-list></note-list>
  </div>
</template>
<script>
  import NoteList from './NoteList.vue';
  import NoteEditor from './NoteEditor.vue';
```

```
export default {
  components: {
    NoteList,
    NoteEditor,
  },
};
</script>
<style>
  // ...
</style>
```

After having added some CSS to the components and restyling the application a bit, it now looks like the following figure:

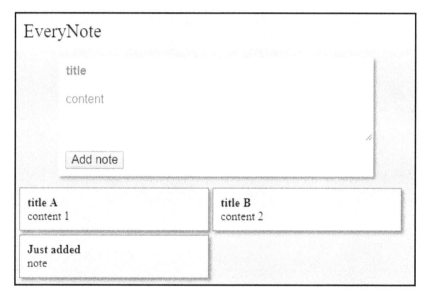

Figure 3.4: EveryNote restyled

You can download the code at this stage by typing the following:

```
git checkout step-2_create-notes
```

Deleting existing notes

The next feature I am going to implement is the ability to delete notes. The following is the updated To-do list:

```
To-do:
Delete a note*
- delete action
- delete mutation
- create Note component and use it in NoteList component

Update an existing note
Save notes to LocalStorage

Extra:
Search among notes
Pin a note

Done:
Show all notes
Create new notes
```

In order to let users delete notes, I need to update the note frame to have a **delete** button, add a deleteNote action, and add a DELETE_NOTE mutation. Finally, I will extract the note frame code from NoteList and create a Note component. Let's create the DELETE_NOTE mutation.

Test code:

```
// test/store/mutations.spec.js
import { mutations, types } from '../../src/store/mutations';

describe('EveryNote root mutations', () => {
  // ...

  it('should delete a note', () => {
    const DELETE_NOTE = mutations[types.DELETE_NOTE];
    const aNote = {};
    const state = { noteList: [aNote] };

    DELETE_NOTE(state, aNote);

    expect(state.noteList.length).toBe(0);
  });

  it('should NOT delete a note if not inside noteList', ()=>{
    const DELETE_NOTE = mutations[types.DELETE_NOTE];
```

```
      const aNote = {};
      const state = { noteList: [aNote] };
      const anotherNote = {};

      DELETE_NOTE(state, anotherNote);

      expect(state.noteList.length).toBe(1);
    });
  });
```

Application code:

```
// src/store/mutations.js
export const types = {
  UPDATE_CURRENT_NOTE: 'UPDATE_CURRENT_NOTE',
  ADD_NOTE: 'ADD_NOTE',
  DELETE_NOTE: 'DELETE_NOTE',
};

export const mutations = {
  // ...
  [types.DELETE_NOTE](state, aNote) {
    const index = state.noteList.indexOf(aNote);
    if (index >= 0) {
      state.noteList.splice(index, 1);
    }
  },
};
```

Then let's add `deleteNote` to the actions.

Test code:

```
// test/store/actions.spec.js
import actions from '../../src/store/actions';
import { types } from '../../src/store/mutations';

describe('EveryNote root actions', () => {
  // ..
  it('should have deleteNote action', () => {
    const { deleteNote } = actions;
    const mockContext = {
      commit: jasmine.createSpy('commit'),
    };
    const aNote = {};

    deleteNote(mockContext, aNote);
```

```
    expect(mockContext.commit)
      .toHaveBeenCalledWith(types.DELETE_NOTE, aNote);
  });
});
```

Application code:

```
// src/store/actions
import { types } from './mutations';

export default {
  // ...
  deleteNote({ commit }, aNote) {
    commit(types.DELETE_NOTE, aNote);
  },
};
```

Now let's refactor the `NoteList` component to use a new component named `Note`:

```
// src/components/NoteList.vue
<template>
  <div class="container">
    <note v-for="(note, i) in notes" :note="note" :key="i">
    </note>
  </div>
</template>
<script>
  // ...
</script>
<style scoped>
  // ...
```

Then we move the test of the note rendering from the `NoteList` to the `Note` component:

```
// test/components/Note.spec.js
import Vue from 'vue';
import Vuex from 'vuex';
import Note from '../../src/components/Note.vue';

describe('Note.vue', () => {
  let note;
  let store;
  beforeEach(() => {
    Vue.use(Vuex);
    note = { title: 'title', content: 'content' };
  });

  function newNoteCmp() {
```

```
        const Constructor = Vue.extend(Note);
        store = new Vuex.Store({
          state: {},
        });
        return new Constructor({
          propsData: { note },
          store,
        }).$mount();
      }

      it('should render a note', () => {
        const { title, content } = note;

        const noteCmp = newNoteCmp();

        const { $el } = noteCmp;
        const titleEl = $el.querySelector('.title');
        const contentEl = $el.querySelector('.content');
        expect(titleEl.textContent.trim()).toBe(title);
        expect(contentEl.textContent.trim()).toBe(content);
      });
    });
```

Next, let's write the new `Note` component:

```
// src/components/Note.vue
<template>
  <div class="note">
    <div class="title">{{note.title}}</div>
    <div class="content" v-text="note.content"></div>
  </div>
</template>
<script>
  export default {
    props: ['note'],
  };
</script>
<style scoped>
  /* ... */
</style>
```

Finally, we can add a delete button to the `Note` component, which will dispatch a `deleteNote` action upon being clicked:

```
// test/components/Note.spec.js
import Vue from 'vue';
import Vuex from 'vuex';
import Note from '../../src/components/Note.vue';
```

```
describe('Note.vue', () => {
  let note;
  let store;
  beforeEach(() => {
    Vue.use(Vuex);
    note = { title: 'title', content: 'content' };
  });

  function newNoteCmp() {
    // ...
  }

  it('should render a note', () => {
    // ...
  });

  it('should emit deleteNote on delete tap', () => {
    const noteCmp = newNoteCmp();
    spyOn(store, 'dispatch');

    noteCmp.onDelete();

    expect(store.dispatch)
      .toHaveBeenCalledWith('deleteNote', note);
  });
});
```

Following is the updated Note.vue code that will make the test pass:

```
// src/components/Note.vue
<template>
  <div class="note">
    <div class="title">{{note.title}}</div>
    <div class="content" v-text="note.content">
    </div>
    <div class="icons">
      <img class="delete" src="./delete.svg"
           @click="onDelete"/>
    </div>
  </div>
</template>
<script>
  export default {
    props: ['note'],
    methods: {
      onDelete() {
        this.$store.dispatch('deleteNote', this.note);
      },
```

```
    },
  };
</script>
<style scoped>
  // ...
</style>
```

In order to run the preceding code, you need a `delete.svg` file. You can find it in the Git repository of this book, or you can use another image.

You can download the code at this stage by typing the following:

```
git checkout step-3_delete-notes
```

Updating existing notes

In order to edit an existing note, we could reuse the `NoteEditor` component. Right now, this component is linked to the `currentNote` property of the main store, but we could use a property to pass the note to be edited, thereby removing its dependency from the main store. This kind of generalization is common while developing Vuex applications, and often leads to two kinds of components:

- **Dumb components**: These do not alter or handle application states; they just receive input through properties and dispatch events
- **Smart components**: These serve as containers for the dumb components; they handle interactions between child components and are dependent on Vuex elements, such as application states and actions

A dumb component should be designed to be reusable, whereas a smart component should be designed to be application dependent.

`NoteEditor` can be refactored into a `dumb` component, letting its parent link it to the application's state.

I noted down these considerations on the `To-do` list:

```
To-do:
Update an existing note*
- re-use NoteEditor with an existing note

Considerations:
- NoteList could be refactored into a dumb component

Save notes to LocalStorage
```

```
Extra:
Search among notes
Pin a note

Done:
Show all notes
Create new notes
Delete a note
```

As you may have noticed, I am also considering transforming `NoteList` into a dumb component so that it can be used to show different lists of notes, such as the pinned notes or the notes that match certain search keywords.

Let's start by refactoring `NoteEditor` into a `dumb` component:

```js
// test/components/NoteEditor.spec.js
import Vue from 'vue';
import NoteEditor from '../../src/components/NoteEditor.vue';

describe('NoteEditor component', () => {
  let note;

  function newNoteEditorCmp() {
    const Constructor = Vue.extend(NoteEditor);
    return new Constructor({
      propsData: { note },
    }).$mount();
  }

  beforeEach(() => {
    note = { title: 'title', content: 'content' };
  });

  it('should init title and content to note prop', () => {
    const editorCmp = newNoteEditorCmp();

    expect(editorCmp.title).not.toBe(undefined);
    expect(editorCmp.title).toBe(note.title);
    expect(editorCmp.content).not.toBe(undefined);
    expect(editorCmp.content).toBe(note.content);
  });

  it('should have onEditDone method ' +
    'that emits the edited note', () => {
    const editorCmp = newNoteEditorCmp();
    spyOn(editorCmp, '$emit');
    const newNote = { title: 'a', content: 'b' };
```

```
    editorCmp.title = newNote.title;
    editorCmp.content = newNote.content;
    editorCmp.onEditDone();

    expect(editorCmp.$emit)
      .toHaveBeenCalledWith('editDone', newNote);
  });

  it('should not emit empty notes', () => {
    note.title = '';
    note.content = '';
    const editorCmp = newNoteEditorCmp();
    spyOn(editorCmp, '$emit');

    editorCmp.onEditDone();

    expect(editorCmp.$emit).not.toHaveBeenCalled();
  });

  it('should reset title, content after onEditDone', () => {
    const editorCmp = newNoteEditorCmp();

    editorCmp.onEditDone();

    expect(editorCmp.title).toBe('');
    expect(editorCmp.content).toBe('');
  });
});
```

As you can see, the tests do not need to use Vuex anymore, and the tests regarding the `currentNote` state property will be moved to its container, which will be developed just after this component.

Also, I decided not to test the `<template>` part of `NoteEditor.vue` because the views change often, and I don't want the tests to slow me down when changing some part of the UI. In my opinion, it is better to reduce the number of unit tests regarding the UI to very few or none. Remember that TDD is about writing code, not about testing existing code. You can write automated tests on a piece of UI when that piece has settled down and is unlikely to change soon. If you agree with me on not testing the views, remember to avoid putting a lot of logic in the `<template>` part of a Vue component.

The new `NoteEditor` implementation looks like the following:

```
// src/components/NoteEditor.vue
<template>
  <div class="container">
    <div class="centered">
      <input v-model="title" type="text" class="title"
             placeholder="title"/><br>
      <textarea v-model="content" class="content"
                rows="3" placeholder="content"></textarea><br>
      <div class="buttons">
        <button @click="onEditDone" class="done">Done</button>
      </div>
    </div>
  </div>
</template>
<script>
  export default {
    props: ['note'],
    data() {
      return {
        title: this.note.title,
        content: this.note.content,
      };
    },
    methods: {
      onEditDone() {
        if (this.title !== '' || this.content !== '') {
          this.$emit('editDone', {
            title: this.title,
            content: this.content,
          });
        }
        this.title = '';
        this.content = '';
      },
    },
  };
</script>
<style scoped>
  // ...
</style>
```

We now need a container for this component, which is the `App.vue` component, plus the code that links `NoteEditor` to the `currentNote` state property:

```javascript
// test/components/App.spec.js
import Vue from 'vue';
import Vuex from 'vuex';
import App from '../../src/components/App.vue';

describe('App.vue', () => {
  let store;
  let noteList;
  let currentNote;

  function newAppCmp() {
    const Constructor = Vue.extend(App);
    store = new Vuex.Store({
      state: { currentNote, noteList },
    });

    return new Constructor({
      store,
    }).$mount();
  }

  beforeEach(() => {
    Vue.use(Vuex);
    noteList = [];
    currentNote = { title: '', content: '' };
  });

  it('should update store.currentNote ' +
    'on onAddDone event', () => {
    const app = newAppCmp();
    spyOn(app.$store, 'dispatch');
    const aNote = {};

    app.onAddDone(aNote);

    expect(app.$store.dispatch)
      .toHaveBeenCalledWith('addNote', aNote);
  });
});
```

Following is the code that will make the test pass:

```
// src/components/App.vue
<template>
  <div class="app">
    <div class="header">EveryNote</div>
    <div class="body">
      <note-editor :note="$store.state.currentNote"
                   @editDone="onAddDone"/>
      <note-list/>
    </div>
  </div>
</template>
<script>
  import NoteList from './NoteList.vue';
  import NoteEditor from './NoteEditor.vue';

  export default {
    components: {
      NoteList,
      NoteEditor,
    },
    methods: {
      onAddDone(note) {
        this.$store.dispatch('addNote', note);
      },
    },
  };
</script>
<style scoped>
  // ...
</style>
```

Finally, we need the `editNote` and `updateNote` actions and the corresponding mutations. The first one will set the current note under editing and the last one will persist changes to the note we just edited.

Test code:

```
// src/store/actions
import { types } from './mutations';

export default {
  addNote({ commit }, aNote) {
    commit(types.ADD_NOTE, aNote);
  },
  deleteNote({ commit }, aNote) {
```

```
      commit(types.DELETE_NOTE, aNote);
    },
    editNote({ commit }, aNote) {
      commit(types.EDIT_NOTE, aNote);
    },
    updateNote({ commit }, aNote) {
      commit(types.UPDATE_NOTE, aNote);
    },
};
```

Application code:

```
// src/store/mutations.js
export const types = {
  UPDATE_CURRENT_NOTE: 'UPDATE_CURRENT_NOTE',
  ADD_NOTE: 'ADD_NOTE',
  DELETE_NOTE: 'DELETE_NOTE',
  EDIT_NOTE: 'EDIT_NOTE',
  UPDATE_NOTE: 'UPDATE_NOTE',
};

export const mutations = {
  // ...
  [types.EDIT_NOTE](state, aNote) {
    const index = state.noteList.indexOf(aNote);
    if (index >= 0) {
      state.editIndex = index;
      state.editNote = state.noteList[index];
    }
  },
  [types.UPDATE_NOTE](state, aNote) {
    const index = state.editIndex;
    if (index >= 0) {
      state.editNote = null;
      state.noteList.splice(index, 1, aNote);
      state.editIndex = -1;
    }
  },
};
```

The tests are similar to the other action tests that we completed, so I will not repeat them.

The last step is to update the Note component to dispatch an editNote action when the user presses the edit icon of a note:

```
// src/components/Note.ue
<template>
  <div class="note">
```

```
        <div class="title">{{note.title}}</div>
        <div class="content"
            style="white-space: pre-line;" v-text="note.content">
        </div>
        <div class="icons">
          <img class="edit" src="./edit.svg"
              @click="onEdit"/>
          <img class="delete" src="./delete.svg"
              @click="onDelete"/>
        </div>
      </div>
    </template>
    <script>
      export default {
        props: ['note'],
        methods: {
          onDelete() {
            this.$store.dispatch('deleteNote', this.note);
          },
          onEdit() {
            this.$store.dispatch('editNote', this.note);
          },
        },
      };
    </script>
    <style scoped>
      // ...
    </style>
```

After that, we modify the App component to show the note to be edited when editNote is dispatched:

```
// src/components/App.vue
<template>
  <div class="app">
    <div class="header">EveryNote</div>
    <div class="body">
      <note-editor :note="$store.state.currentNote"
                  @editDone="onAddDone"/>
      <note-list/>
    </div>
    <div class="overlay" v-if="$store.state.editNote">
      <note-editor class="note-editor" @editDone="onEditDone"
                  :note="$store.state.editNote"/>
    </div>
  </div>
</template>
```

```
<script>
  import NoteList from './NoteList.vue';
  import NoteEditor from './NoteEditor.vue';

  export default {
    components: {
      NoteList,
      NoteEditor,
    },
    methods: {
      onAddDone(note) {
        this.$store.dispatch('addNote', note);
      },
      onEditDone(note) {
        this.$store.dispatch('updateNote', note);
      },
    },
  };
</script>
<style scoped>
  // ...
</style>
```

You can download the code at this stage by typing the following:

```
git checkout step-4_edit-notes
```

Other features

Following is the updated To-do list that shows what we've done and what's remaining:

```
To-do:
Save notes to LocalStorage

Considerations:
- NoteList could be refactored into a dumb component

Extra:
Search among notes
Pin a note

Done:
Show all notes
Create new notes
Delete a note
Update an existing note
```

I will not discuss the other features in this book because I think it is now clear how Vuex development works and how Vuex applications can be tested. You can find the complete application code in the book's repository at `https://github.com/PacktPublishing/-Vuex-Condensed`.

When persisting notes to `localStorage`, instead of saving only the list of notes, we will use a Vuex plugin to save all the application states. You will read about this in the last chapter of this book, which will introduce you to `vuex-persistedstate`, a plugin to persist the Vuex application state with `localStorage`.

Recap and some considerations

We implemented the so-called CRUD functions, create, read, update, and delete.

The **EveryNote** application, at this stage, looks like the following:

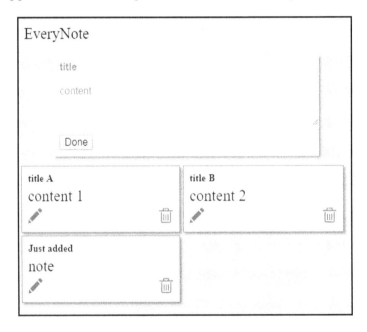

Figure 3.5: EveryNote app with CRUD operations

When tapping on the pencil icon, the note editor opens. The following is a screenshot of the application in editing mode:

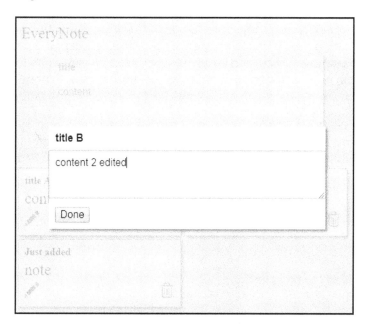

Figure 3.6: EveryNote editing dialog

In order to reach this stage of *EveryNote* development, we used a TDD approach and an incremental design and development process. As I promised in the introduction, I developed this application while writing this chapter. This means that I did not follow an optimal development path—in fact, I had to change some code and even delete some tests. That is normal while developing. At any rate, spend more time during the design phase in order to avoid architectural mistakes and save time during the development phase. In fact, a good design is fundamental, but it is also important not to go into too much detail while in this phase. Sometimes, people think that TDD bypasses design. That's completely false—in fact, you will pay twice for a mistake: Once in the production code and once in the test code.

Synchronizing with a remote server

While developing the *EveryNote* application, I decided to write an action for each mutation. If an action only commits a mutation, you may avoid writing this action and commit the corresponding mutation inside the components. Like Google Keep, the *EveryNote* application can be empowered by persisting notes to a remote server so that a user can read his or her notes from any computer or mobile device. In that case, actions come in handy because they can perform asynchronous operations to keep the application state synchronized with a server.

I will not implement the code to persist the application state with a remote server, but I would like to show you an example of how the list of notes can be fetched from a remote server when the app gets loaded.

The idea is that when `App.vue` is loaded, we can fire a `loadNotesFromServer` action that will update the saved state into the `localStorage` with the list of notes from the server.

Let's start with the `loadNotesFromServer` action tests:

```
// test/store/actions.spec.js
import actions from '../../src/store/actions';
import { types } from '../../src/store/mutations';
import api from '../../src/api/api-mock';

describe('EveryNote root actions', () => {
  // ...

  it('should have loadNotesFromServer action', (done) => {
    const { loadNotesFromServer } = actions;
    const mockContext = {
      commit: jasmine.createSpy('commit'),
    };
    const aNote = {};
    spyOn(api, 'fetchAllNotes').and.returnValue(Promise.resolve([aNote]));

    loadNotesFromServer(mockContext).then(() => {
      expect(mockContext.commit)
        .toHaveBeenCalledWith(types.ADD_NOTE, aNote);
      done();
    });
  });
});
```

The action code is as follows:

```
// src/store/actions.js
import { types } from './mutations';
import api from '../api/api-mock';

export default {
  // ...
  loadNotesFromServer({ commit }) {
    return api.fetchAllNotes().then((notes) => {
      notes.forEach(note => commit(types.ADD_NOTE, note));
    });
  },
};
```

It is a simplistic implementation—in a real case, you may need to merge the list of notes from the server with the notes saved in the `localStorage`.

Then, we alter `App.vue` to dispatch the action:

```
// src/components/App.vue
<template>
  // ..
</template>
<script>
  import NoteList from './NoteList.vue';
  import NoteEditor from './NoteEditor.vue';

  export default {
    created() {
      this.$store.dispatch('loadNotesFromServer');
    },
    components: {
      NoteList,
      NoteEditor,
    },
    methods: {
      // ...
    },
  };
</script>
<style scoped>
  // ...
</style>
```

Finally, we create a mock implementation of the API, moving the two notes from the store to the mock API:

```
// src/api/api-mock.js
export default {
  fetchAllNotes() {
    return Promise.resolve([
      { title: 'title A', content: 'content 1' },
      { title: 'title B', content: 'content 2' },
    ]);
  },
};
```

You can download the code at this stage by typing the following:

```
git checkout step-5_remote-mock-server
```

Summary

In this chapter, we developed the *EveryNote* application, going through the Vuex concepts and looking at how to use Vuex in a real application's development. We also looked at the TDD basics and saw how Vue/Vuex elements can be tested.

But what about debugging? Even with tests, a debug is sometimes needed. The next chapter will explain how web applications can be debugged using browser developer tools, as well as how to use `vue-devtools` to easily debug Vue/Vuex applications.

Debugging Vuex Applications

5

By developing your applications using test-driven development, you will reduce debugging time considerably. Still, there are moments when a piece of code refuses to work as expected or a subtle bug hides among your code.

Fortunately, browsers provide developer tools to help frontend developers debug their applications and Vue provides vue-devtools .

In the following chapter, we will learn about:

- Using vue-devtools
- Using the built-in logger plugin

 To understand this chapter, you need to have basic knowledge of the Chrome developer Tools instrument.

Using vue-devtools

Vue.js provides the vue-devtools utility to help programmers debug Vue applications. Vuex enhances this tool to keep track of every mutation committed.

You can install this utility as an extension for Chrome or FireFox, or you can navigate to `https://github.com/vuejs/vue-devtools` for instructions on how to install it.

Start the *EveryNote* application by typing `npm start`, open Google Chrome with vue-devtools installed at `http://localhost:8080/`, then press *F12*.

Component inspector

If you select the **Elements** tab in Chrome Developer Tools, you will see something like the following screenshot:

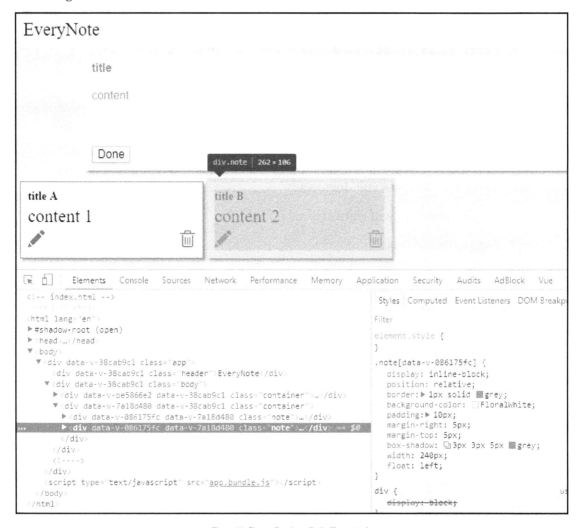

Figure 4.1: Chrome Developer Tools, Elements tab

Below the **Elements** tab, you can see the current DOM tree of the *EveryNote* application. The selected `div` is the element containing the second note.

By mapping the DOM structure back to the Vue components we've just coded, you can understand that the selected element is the root element of the component `Note`. Wouldn't it be better to see something like `<Note>` instead of the detailed `Note` DOM elements structure?

Now select the **Vue** tab, and you will see something like the following screenshot:

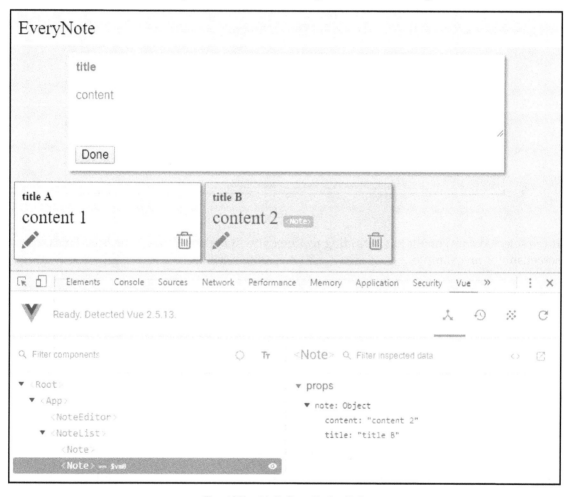

Figure 4.2: Vue tab inside Chrome Developer Tools.

In a glance, you can see the application structure with the components' names instead of the components' DOM elements. By moving the mouse over the components, the corresponding element will be highlighted in the HTML page. If you press the select button (⬡), you can select an element inside the HTML page and have it highlighted in the components tree.

By selecting an element from the tree below the **Filter components** box, you will also see its properties in the props frame, as shown in the following screenshot:

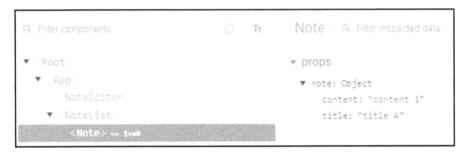

Figure 4.3: Props frame

If the selected component has a binding to Vuex, it will appear in the same box. This next screenshot is an example:

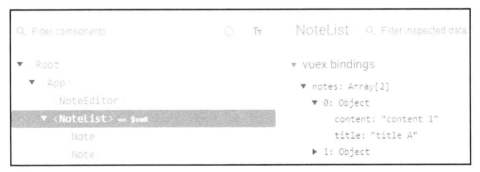

Figure 4.4: Vuex component bindings

This way, it becomes easy to move across Vue components inside a page, and see their state.

The next feature we will see is the events inspector.

Events inspector

Watching the components state is useful, but wouldn't it be great if we could also record the interaction between components? In fact, vue-devtools provides two other features: events and Vuex mutation recording.

In the following screenshot, you can see the **Filter events** section of vue-devtools:

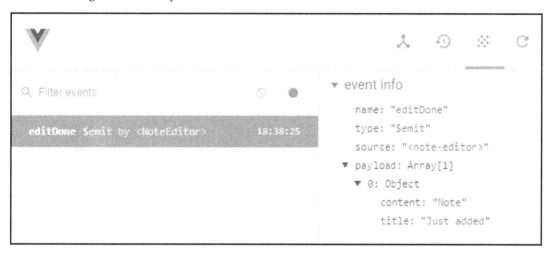

Figure 4.5: Filter events section

As an example, I added a note and, because of this action, the **Filter events** tab recorded that an `editDone` event has been fired inside `NoteEditor`. It also shows the event payload.

Finally, we will explore a **Vuex** dedicated tab.

Vuex time travel

By moving to the Vuex section by pressing the Vue button 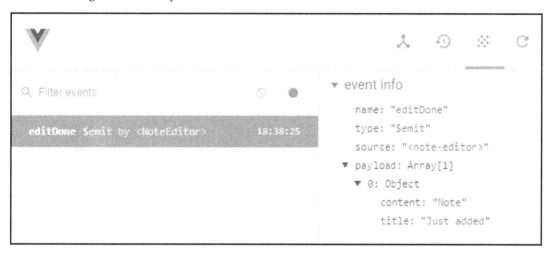, you will be able to record all the Vuex mutations committed. The following screenshot shows this feature:

Figure 4.6: Vuex time travel tab

As you can see, after the application has been loaded, two notes have been added. Those are the notes that get added because of the fake call to a hypothetical server, triggered by the action `loadNotesFromServer`.

After that, I clicked the Delete button of the second note. In fact, the third mutation recorded is DELETE_NOTE. You can see the state and the mutation payload for each mutation, and even undo a commit, as demonstrated in the following screenshot, where I am about to undo the DELETE_NOTE mutation:

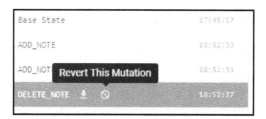

Figure 4.7: Undoing the DELETE_NOTE mutation

As a result of the undo, the application state reverts to the previous mutation, and the application shows the second note again, as shown in the following screenshot:

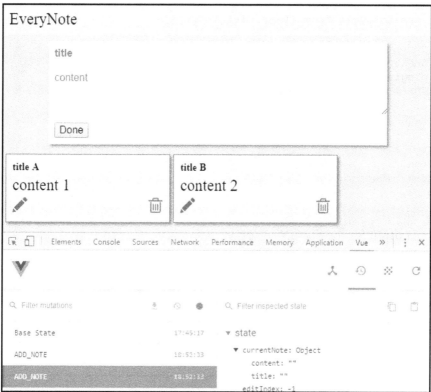

Figure 4.8: Application state after undoing the DELETE_NOTE mutation.

The ability of undo mutations comes in handy when you want to debug an action and the corresponding mutation: you can put a breakpoint in the action code using the **Sources** tab in Chrome Developer Tools, and then execute and rollback the mutation as many times as you need. Note that, if you use Chrome debugger to restart the **Action** code after a mutation has been committed, then the application state has already been changed, and the second execution is influenced by the new state. On the contrary, if you undo a commit, you can safely re-execute a piece of code without the need to reload the entire page.

Finally, the two buttons above the **state** frame let you export and import the application state from and to the clipboard.

Enabling the Vuex built-in logger plugin

Vuex provides a built-in plugin to log every mutation. It can be added to the application store as follows:

```
// src/store/index.js
import createLogger from 'vuex/dist/logger';
// ...

const debug = process.env.NODE_ENV !== 'production';
const plugins = debug ? [createLogger({})] : [];
const store = new Vuex.Store({
  state: {
   // ...
  },
  mutations,
  actions,
  strict: debug,
  plugins,
});
```

The resulting output for the *EveryNote* app is:

```
▶ mutation ADD_NOTE @ 09:47:16.688
▶ mutation ADD_NOTE @ 09:47:16.698
▼ mutation DELETE_NOTE @ 10:02:08.010
    prev state ▶ {noteList: Array(2), currentNote: {…}, editNote: null, editIndex: -1}
    mutation ▶ {type: "DELETE_NOTE", payload: {…}}
    next state ▶ {noteList: Array(1), currentNote: {…}, editNote: null, editIndex: -1}
  > |
```

Figure 4.8: Vuex built-in logger plugin

As you can see in the preceding screenshot, it logs not only the mutation name but also the previous and next state.

You can download the code at this stage by typing:

```
git checkout step-6_vuex-built-in-logger
```

Summary

In this chapter, we went through vue-devtools features, and we introduced the Vuex built-in logger plugin. But what exactly is a Vuex plugin?

Well, that is the topic of `Chapter 5`, *Using the Vuex Plugin System*; in the next few pages, we will learn what a Vuex plugin is, and how we can write a custom one.

Using the Vuex Plugin System

6

In previous chapters, I wrote about the possibility of persisting the *EveryNote* application state, using the Vuex plugin system. We also learned about a built-in logger plugin to log every mutation. But, what exactly is a Vuex plugin? And how can we write a custom plugin?

In the following pages, you will:

- Learn about the Vuex plugin system
- Add two useful plugins to the *EveryNote* application
- Write a Google Analytics plugin to track user interaction with your app
- Develop an undo/redo plugin

Technical requirements

You will be required to have Node.js installed on a system. Finally, to use the Git repository of this book, the user needs to install Git.

The code files of this chapter can be found on GitHub:
https://github.com/PacktPublishing/Vuex-Quick-Start-Guide/tree/master/chapter-6
https://github.com/PacktPublishing/Vuex-Quick-Start-Guide/tree/master/chapter-6-promises

Check out the following video to see the code in action:
https://goo.gl/aZjE63

Understanding the Vuex plugin system

A Vuex plugin is a function that receives the application store as the only argument and can subscribe to mutations.

The following is an example of a plugin:

```
const consolePlugin = (store) => {
store.subscribe((mutation, state) => {
    // called after every mutation.
    // The mutation comes in the format of { type, payload }.
    console.log(mutation, state);
  });
};
```

You can add a plugin to the store as follows:

```
const store = new Vuex.Store({
  // ...
  plugins: [consolePlugin]
});
```

Like components, plugins cannot directly alter the state; they have to commit a mutation.

For example, imagine that we want to show the last time a mutation has been committed. We could write a plugin as follows:

```
// src/store/plugins.js
// ...
const lastEditDate = (store) => {
  store.subscribe((mutation) => {
    if (mutation.type !== types.UPDATE_LAST_EDIT_DATE) {
      store.commit(types.UPDATE_LAST_EDIT_DATE);
    }
  });
};
```

Since we can subscribe to every mutation receiving the new state, we could persist the application state with `localStorage`. In fact, there is a plugin called `vuex-persistedstate` that does exactly that. You can read more about this plugin in the following pages.

Empowering EveryNote with two plugins

If you Google *Vuex plugins*, you may find various plugins for different purposes. I selected two that you will probably want to use in your next Vuex project. These plugins are:

- vuex-persistedstate
- vuex-router-sync

We are going to use the first one to save the EveryNote state with `localStorage`, so that we don't lose all the notes every time the browser page is reloaded.

It is strongly recommended that you use the second one, vuex-router-sync, if you are creating a single-page web application. In this case, you are already using vue-router and vuex-router-sync will synchronize the current route, as part of Vuex store's state.

Saving the app state with vuex-persistedstate

The *EveryNote* application currently shows two fake notes and loses newly created notes every time you reload the page. By adding the `vuex-persistedstate` plugin, notes will be saved with `localStorage`.

To add the `vuex-persistedstate` type, enter the following:

```
npm install --save vuex-persistedstate
```

After that, we need to add it to the plugins list:

```js
// src/store/index.js
// ...
import createPersistedState from 'vuex-persistedstate';
// ...

plugins.push(createPersistedState());
const store = new Vuex.Store({
  state: {
   // ...
  },
  mutations,
  actions,
  strict: debug,
  plugins,
});
```

Finally, we need to remove the two fake notes from the mock API:

```js
// src/api/api-mock.js
export default {
  fetchAllNotes() {
    return Promise.resolve([]);
  },
};
```

From now on, if you add a note and then reload the page, that note will still be there.

`vuex-persistedstate` is highly configurable and can persist the application state to every synchronous storage. For example, you can configure it to use `sessionStorage`, instead of `localStorage`, if you want the state to be reset when the application page is closed.

You can find more information at: `https://github.com/robinvdvleuten/vuex-persistedstate`.

Synchronizing router data with vuex-router-sync

If you are using vue-router in your application, you may also want to use vuex-router-sync because, as it says on the plugin website, *it syncs vue-router's current $route as part of vuex store's state.*

To install this plugin, type:

```
npm install vuex-router-sync --save
```

To add it to the *EveryNote* app, you need to add vue-router to the project:

```
npm install vue-router --save
```

and modify `src/store/index.js` as follows:

```
// src/store/index.js
import { sync } from 'vuex-router-sync';
// ...

const store = new Vuex.Store({
  state: {
   // ...
  },
  mutations,
  actions,
  strict: debug,
  plugins,
});

sync(store, router);
// ...
```

But how does it work? Each time the route changes, this plugin updates the `store.state.route` property. This property consists of:

```
store.state.route.path // current path (string)
store.state.route.params // current params (object)
store.state.route.query // current query (object)
```

To update the store property, it commits a `route.ROUTE_CHANGED` mutation, where `route` is the default name of the module of the vuex-router-sync plugin.

You can change the module name it uses as follows:

```
sync(store, router, { moduleName: 'CustomRouteSyncModule' } );
```

In order to programmatically change a route, use vue-router; do not modify `store.state.route`.

You can find more information at: `https://github.com/vuejs/vuex-router-sync`.

In the following pages, we are going to develop a Google Analytics plugin that uses vuex-router-sync to send page-views to Google servers.

Developing a Google Analytics plugin

In the following pages, I will assume that you are familiar with Google Analytics and that you have correctly configured Google Analytics tracking in your application. If not, you can Google it, understand how it works, and come back here. A basic understanding is more than enough to proceed with the following pages.

The first step is to add this Google Analytics tracking code snippet to the `index.html` file:

```
<!-- index.html -->

<!-- Global site tag (gtag.js) - Google Analytics -->
<script async
src="https://www.googletagmanager.com/gtag/js?id=GA_TRACKING_ID"></script>
<script>
  window.dataLayer = window.dataLayer || [];
  function gtag(){dataLayer.push(arguments);}
  gtag('js', new Date());

  gtag('config', 'GA_TRACKING_ID');
</script>
```

After that, a global `gtag(...)` function will be available to send events to Google Analytics servers.

Typically, an application tracks page views and some events. To send an event to Google Analytics servers, it is enough to write:

```
gtag('event', 'MUTATION_NAME');
```

Using the preceding code, we can write a plugin that sends an Analytics event for each mutation, as follows:

```
// src/store/plugins.js
// ...
export const googleAnalytics = (store) => {
  store.subscribe((mutation) => {
    gtag('event', mutation.type);
  });
};
```

In order to send page views, we can exploit the vuex-router-sync `route.ROUTE_CHANGED` mutation committed every time the location changes.

We can update the Analytics plugin accordingly, as follows:

```
// src/store/plugins.js
import analytics from '../gtag';
// ...
export const googleAnalytics = (store) => {
  store.subscribe((mutation, state) => {
    if (mutation.type === 'route/ROUTE_CHANGED') {
      analytics.sendPageView(state.route.path);
    } else {
      analytics.sendEvent(mutation.type);
    }
  });
};
```

Where the `analytics` object is something like:

```
// src/gtag/index.js
const GA_TRACKING_ID = 'GA_TRACKING_ID';

class GtagAnalytics {
  static sendEvent(action) {
    gtag('event', action);
  }
```

```
  static sendPageView(pagePath) {
    gtag('config', GA_TRACKING_ID, { page_path: pagePath });
  }
}

export default GtagAnalytics;
```

You probably do not want to send all mutations as analytics events; in that case, you can create a map of mutation types that you want to send, or a list of mutation types you don't want to be sent.

You can download the EveryNote code with the Google Analytics plugin by typing:

```
git checkout chapter-5/step-7_google-analytics-plugin
```

Developing an undo/redo plugin

The Google Analytics plugin we just coded is a good and simple example of how the Vuex plugin system can be exploited to add features to your application, without touching the application core code. But what about a more complex plugin? Is the Vuex plugin also suited for more complex operations? Well, of course, it is! In the following pages, we will develop an undo/redo plugin, which is still a simple, but not trivial example.

We can exploit the fact that, in using the Vuex system, we have a single centralized state and this state can only be modified by mutations. The idea is to take a snapshot of the state each time it gets modified. Then, to go back in the mutation history, it is enough to set the current state to a snapshot, representing an older state before the mutation occurred.

Let's start by creating a plugin that registers a module called undoRedo:

```
store.registerModule(moduleName, {
  namespaced: true,
  getters: {
    canUndo() {}, // Tells if undo can be performed
    canRedo() {}, // Tells if redo can be performed
  },
  state: {
    currentPosition: 0, // Position in the history
    snapshots: [], // Snapshots taken
  },
  mutations: {
    [UNDO]() {}, // Mutation to undo last mutation
    [REDO](state) {}, // Mutation to redo last mutation
    [UPDATE_CURRENT_POSITION](){},//update currentPosition
```

```
    [UPDATE_SNAPSHOTS](){}, //update snapshots
  },
});
```

In the preceding code, we define two state properties:

- **currentPosition**: This represents the index of the current snapshot. When an undo mutation is committed, we decrease the index; when a redo mutation or another one is committed, the index is increased.
- **snapshots**: This is an array containing state snapshots.

After that, we need two corresponding mutations to update these properties, as well as an UNDO and a REDO mutation to actually let plugin clients undo or redo modifications.

Finally, we provide two getters, canUndo() and canRedo(), to expose the undoable/redoable state of the plugin.

We can now subscribe to mutations to take a snapshot each time the application state gets changed:

```
const undoRedoPlugin = (store) => {
  function takeStateSnapshot(state) {
    // ...
  }

  function restoreStateSnapshot(state, toRestore) {
    // ...
  }

  store.subscribe(({ type }, state) => {
    if (mutationsToExclude[type] === undefined) {
      const index = state[moduleName].currentPosition + 1;
      const snapshots = state[moduleName].snapshots.slice();
      snapshots.length = index + 1;
      snapshots[index] = takeStateSnapshot(state);
      store.commit(currentPositionType, index);
      store.commit(updateSnapshotType, snapshots);
    }
  });

  store.registerModule(moduleName, {
    // ...
  });
};
```

Of course, there are mutations that must be excluded, such as mutations of snapshots or currentPosition properties, and mutations that a user of this plugin may want to exclude, such as route/ROUTE_CHANGED if vuex-router-sync is used in the application.

We can now implement the undo/redo mutations as follows:

```
store.registerModule(moduleName, {
  namespaced: true,
  getters: {
    canUndo({ currentPosition }) {
      return currentPosition >= 1;
    },
    canRedo({ currentPosition, snapshots }) {
      return currentPosition < snapshots.length - 1;
    },
  },
  state: {
    currentPosition: 0,
    snapshots: [takeStateSnapshot(store.state)],
  },
  mutations: {
    [UNDO](state) {
      if (store.getters[canUndoGetter]) {
        state.currentPosition--;
        const { snapshots } = state;
        const snapShot = snapshots[state.currentPosition];
        restoreStateSnapshot(store.state, snapShot);
      }
    },
    [REDO](state) {
      if (store.getters[canRedoGetter]) {
        state.currentPosition++;
        const { snapshots } = state;
        const snapShot = snapshots[state.currentPosition];
        restoreStateSnapshot(store.state, snapShot);
      }
    },
    [UPDATE_CURRENT_POSITION](state, value) {
      state.currentPosition = value;
    },
    [UPDATE_SNAPSHOTS](state, value) {
      state.snapshots = value;
    },
  },
});
```

As you can see, the preceding code is just about restoring the right snapshot.

When taking a snapshot, not every state property should be considered and each snapshot must be a copy of the state. The following code shows these concepts:

```
function takeStateSnapshot(state) {
  const toClone = {};
  Object.keys(state).forEach((key) => {
    if (statePropsToExclude[key] === undefined) {
      toClone[key] = state[key];
    }
  });

  return JSON.stringify(toClone);
}

function restoreStateSnapshot(state, toRestore) {
  const clone = JSON.parse(toRestore);
  Object.keys(clone).forEach((key) => {
    state[key] = clone[key];
  });
}
```

Finally, we can provide a factory method to create and configure the undo/redo plugin. The following is the entire plugin code:

```
// src/store/undo-redo-plugin.js
export default (options) => {
  const moduleName = 'undoRedo' || options.moduleName;
  const UNDO = 'undo';
  const REDO = 'redo';
  const UPDATE_CURRENT_POSITION = 'UPDATE_CURRENT_POSITION';
  const UPDATE_SNAPSHOTS = 'UPDATE_SNAPSHOTS';
  const undoType = `${moduleName}/${UNDO}`;
  const redoType = `${moduleName}/${REDO}`;
  const currentPositionType =
    `${moduleName}/${UPDATE_CURRENT_POSITION}`;
  const updateSnapshotType =
    `${moduleName}/${UPDATE_SNAPSHOTS}`;
  const canUndoGetter = `${moduleName}/canUndo`;
  const canRedoGetter = `${moduleName}/canRedo`;

  const statePropsToExclude = {
    [moduleName]: '',
  };
  if (options.statePropsToExclude) {
    options.statePropsToExclude.forEach((toExclude) => {
```

```
      statePropsToExclude[toExclude] = '';
  });
}

const mutationsToExclude = {
  [undoType]: '',
  [redoType]: '',
  [currentPositionType]: '',
  [updateSnapshotType]: '',
};
if (options.mutationsToExclude) {
  options.mutationsToExclude.forEach((toExclude) => {
    mutationsToExclude[toExclude] = '';
  });
}

const undoRedoPlugin = (store) => {
  function takeStateSnapshot(state) {
    const toClone = {};
    Object.keys(state).forEach((key) => {
      if (statePropsToExclude[key] === undefined) {
        toClone[key] = state[key];
      }
    });

    return JSON.stringify(toClone);
  }

  function restoreStateSnapshot(state, toRestore) {
    const clone = JSON.parse(toRestore);
    Object.keys(clone).forEach((key) => {
      state[key] = clone[key];
    });
  }

  store.subscribe(({ type }, state) => {
    if (mutationsToExclude[type] === undefined) {
      const index = state[moduleName].currentPosition + 1;
      const snapshots = state[moduleName].snapshots.slice();
      snapshots.length = index + 1;
      snapshots[index] = takeStateSnapshot(state);
      store.commit(currentPositionType, index);
      store.commit(updateSnapshotType, snapshots);
    }
  });

  store.registerModule(moduleName, {
    namespaced: true,
```

```
    getters: {
      canUndo({ currentPosition }) {
        return currentPosition >= 1;
      },
      canRedo({ currentPosition, snapshots }) {
        return currentPosition < snapshots.length - 1;
      },
    },
    state: {
      currentPosition: 0,
      snapshots: [takeStateSnapshot(store.state)],
    },
    mutations: {
      [UNDO](state) {
        if (store.getters[canUndoGetter]) {
          state.currentPosition--;
          const { snapshots } = state;
          const snapShot = snapshots[state.currentPosition];
          restoreStateSnapshot(store.state, snapShot);
        }
      },
      [REDO](state) {
        if (store.getters[canRedoGetter]) {
          state.currentPosition++;
          const { snapshots } = state;
          const snapShot = snapshots[state.currentPosition];
          restoreStateSnapshot(store.state, snapShot);
        }
      },
      [UPDATE_CURRENT_POSITION](state, value) {
        state.currentPosition = value;
      },
      [UPDATE_SNAPSHOTS](state, value) {
        state.snapshots = value;
      },
    },
  });
};

  return undoRedoPlugin;
};
```

You can download the EveryNote code with the undo/redo plugin, by typing:

```
git checkout chapter-5/step-8_undo-redo-plugin
```

Undo/redo, implemented this way, works well with an application that does not synchronize its state with a server. Normally, it is not enough to restore the previous state, but you need also to perform an action to update the server data. For example, if you undo a delete note, you need to send the undeleted note data to the remote server. This means that a real undo/redo feature is application-dependent, and that the plugin we wrote needs to be extended to also handle synchronization with a remote server.

Dealing with asynchronicity using promises

In a real undo/redo plugin you will probably send data to a server, which is an asynchronous operation. We understood that asynchronicity must be dealt with inside Vuex actions. When you dispatch an action, `store.dispatch('anAction')`, the `dispatch` method returns a `Promise`. In the following pages I will explain how you can handle asynchronous operations using `Promise`, a relatively new JavaScript feature.

Dealing with asynchronous operations in JavaScript can be tricky. I have seen incredibly messy pieces of code just because the programmer didn't know how to deal with asynchronous code.

The worst way of waiting for a piece of data that will be available later is polling. *Never do something like this*:

```
// Just don't use this way!
let dataFromServer;

// ...

const waitForData = () => {
    if(dataFromServer !== undefined) {
        doSomethingWith(dataFromServer);
    } else {
        setTimeout(waitForData, 100);
    }
};
setTimeout(waitForData, 100);
```

The preceding example can be refactored using a callback:

```
api.getDataFromServer((dataFromServer) => {
    // do something with dataFromServer
});
```

Callbacks are good for simple operations, but become quickly unmanageable when you need to combine more than one callback. Have you ever heard of the phrase *callback hell*?

Fortunately, JavaScript now provides `Promise`, a simple way to deal with asynchronous operations. Using a `Promise`, the preceding code can be rewritten as follows:

```
api.getDataFromServer().then(function success(dataFromServer){
    // do something with dataFromServer
}, function fail(error) {
    // Handle the error
});
```

If you are not familiar with promises, google and study them. The following sections will explain how promises can be chained or be executed in parallel, which, in my opinion, is still not well understood by programmers.

Chaining promises

The `store.dispatch('action')` function returns a promise. This allows the programmer to wait for an action to be completed before executing another one.

Let's see an example where an action is dispatched after another one is completed:

```
store.dispatch('action 1').then(() => {
    return store.dispatch('action 2');
}).then(() => {
    store.commit('mutation depending on action 1 and 2');
});
```

The `then(callback)` method of a `Promise` returns another `Promise`, which will be resolved with the value returned by the callback. If the value returned by the callback is itself a `Promise`, it will wait for this second `Promise` to be completed. OK, I know—the first time you hear it, this concept sounds a bit twisted. I will explain promise concatenation in the following examples:

```
// Creates a resolved promise with a return value 'A'
const p1 = Promise.resolve('A');

console.log('start');
// Chaining promises
p1
  .then(result => result + 'B')
  .then(result => asyncEcho(result + 'C')) // wait 1000 ms
  .then(result => console.log(result))
```

```
console.log('end');

function asyncEcho(echoMsg) {
    return new Promise(resolve => {
        setTimeout(() => resolve(echoMsg), 1000);
    });
}
```

The resulting output is as follows:

```
start
end
// after 1000 ms
ABC
```

First, the synchronous code gets executed, printing `start` and `end`, and then the promise chain gets executed. In the middle step of the chain, a promise that is resolved after 1000 ms is returned from the callback. This makes the last `then(...)` of the chain wait for the `asyncEcho(...)` promise to be resolved before it can execute the last callback.

Until the chain promises get resolved, the code execution moves from one `then()` to the other. But what happens when a promise gets rejected? Let's see another example:

```
// Creates a resolved promise
const p1 = Promise.resolve();

// Chaining promises
p1
  .then(() => {console.log(1); return asyncFail();})
  .then(() => console.log(2), // success
        () => console.log('Fail 2')) // fail
  .then(() => {console.log(3); throw 'An error';}, // success
        () => console.log('Fail 3')) // fail
  .then(() => console.log(4), // success
        () =>{console.log('Fail 4');return Promise.reject()})
  .catch(()=> console.log('Catch called'));

function asyncFail() {
    return new Promise((resolve, reject) => {
        setTimeout(reject, 1000);
    });
}
```

The resulting output is as follows:

```
1
Fail 2
3
Fail 4
Catch called
```

Did you get the right output? Or did you expect to see *Fail 3* after the *Fail 2* line? That is a common mistake. Only if an error occurs inside a callback or a rejected promise is returned is the fail callback of the next step of the chain executed. In all other cases, it is the next success callback that gets executed, even if the fail callback of the previous step was executing.

The following figure explains this concept:

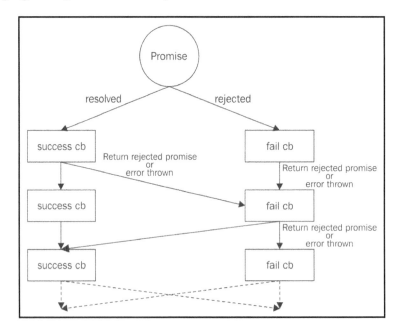

Figure 2.1: Chaining promises

Parallel execution of promises

Now that we know how to chain promises, we also know how to chain Vuex actions since the `store.dispatch(...)` method returns a promise. But what if we want to execute two or more actions in parallel and wait for all of the actions to be completed?

The `Promise` object provides a `Promise.all([p1, p2, ..., pn])` method that returns a promise that is either resolved after all the provided promises are resolved or that is rejected as soon as one of the provided promises is rejected. Let's see an example:

```
const p1 = asyncEcho('A', 500);
const p2 = asyncEcho('B', 1000);
const e = asyncFail('E1', 100);

Promise.all([p1, p2]).then((values) =>
    console.log('OK', values));

Promise.all([p1, p2, e]).then(() => {
  console.log('this gets not executed');
}, (error) => {
  console.log('Err', error);
});

function asyncEcho(echoMsg, delay) {
    return new Promise(resolve => {
        setTimeout(() => resolve(echoMsg), delay);
    });
}

function asyncFail(error, delay) {
    return new Promise((resolve, reject) => {
        setTimeout(() => reject(error), delay);
    });
}
```

The output is as follows:

```
Err E1 // After 100 ms
OK A, B // After 1000 ms
```

Common mistakes when using promises

Finally, let's look at the two common mistakes made when using `Promise`.

The following code shows what happens when a `Promise` constructor callback is misunderstood:

```
console.log(1);
buggyExecuteLater(() => console.log(3));
console.log(2);

function buggyExecuteLater(callback) {
  new Promise(() => callback());
}

// Output
// 1
// 3
// 2
```

The callback function provided to `new Promise(callback)` is executed synchronously. If you want to schedule something immediately after the current JavaScript execution is completed, use `Promise.resolve().then(callback)` or `setTimeout(callback, 0)`.

The following code shows what happens when a programmer forgets to return a rejected promise:

```
function iMayFail() {
  const rand = Math.random();
  const successP = Promise.resolve();
  const failP = Promise.reject();
  return rand < 0.5 ? successP : failP;
}

function buggyToss() {
  return iMayFail().then(
    () => 'Success', // Success callback
    () => 'Fail' // Fail callback
  );
}

buggyToss().then(
  result => console.log('Resolved ' + result),
  result => console.log('Rejected ' + result)
);

// Output is always 'Resolved Fail' or 'Resolved Success'
```

No matter what `Math.random()` returns, the output is always **Resolved Fail or Resolved Success** because the `fail` callback of `buggyToss()` does not throw any error or return a rejected promise. The following is the correct version of `buggyToss()`:

```
function correctToss() {
    return iMayFail().then(
        () => 'Success', // Success callback
        () => Promise.reject('Fail') // Fail callback
    );
}
```

Summary

In this chapter, we looked at how the Vuex plugin system works, we extended the *EveryNote* application with two useful plugins, and we developed two plugins from scratch: a Google Analytics plugin and an undo/redo plugin. Furthermore, generally, we saw how the Vuex plugin system can be exploited to add general features to our application without touching the application's core code.

Finally we understood how to deal with asynchronous operations using JavaScript `Promise` feature.

Other Books You May Enjoy

If you enjoyed this book, you may be interested in these other books by Packt:

Vue.js 2 Design Patterns and Best Practices
Paul Halliday

ISBN: 978-1-78883-979-2

- Understand the theory and patterns of Vue.js
- Build scalable and modular Vue.js applications
- Take advantage of Vuex for reactive state management
- Create single page applications with vue-router
- Use Nuxt for FAST server-side rendered Vue applications
- Convert your application to a Progressive Web App (PWA) and add ServiceWorkers and offline support
- Build your app with Vue.js by following best practices and explore the common anti-patterns to avoid

Full-Stack Vue.js 2 and Laravel 5
Anthony Gore

ISBN: 978-1-78829-958-9

- Core features of Vue.js to create sophisticated user interfaces
- Build a secure backend API with Laravel
- Learn a state-of-the-art web development workflow with Webpack
- Full-stack app design principles and best practices
- Learn to deploy a full-stack app to a cloud server and CDN
- Managing complex application state with Vuex
- Securing a web service with Laravel Passport

Leave a review - let other readers know what you think

Please share your thoughts on this book with others by leaving a review on the site that you bought it from. If you purchased the book from Amazon, please leave us an honest review on this book's Amazon page. This is vital so that other potential readers can see and use your unbiased opinion to make purchasing decisions, we can understand what our customers think about our products, and our authors can see your feedback on the title that they have worked with Packt to create. It will only take a few minutes of your time, but is valuable to other potential customers, our authors, and Packt. Thank you!

Index

M

mapActions helper 39
mapGetters helper 31
mapMutations helper 36
Model 8
model-view-controller (MVC)
  about 7
  issues 8, 9, 10, 11
module
  dynamic registration 44
  local state 41
  reusing 45
  using 39
  with namespace 41
mutation types
  enumerating, with constant strings 34
mutation
  application state, modifying with 31
  committing 32
  committing, with actions 36
  synchronous 35

N

node package manager (npm)
  about 54
  used, to prepare Vue/Vuex project 54, 55, 57,
    59
Node.js
  URL 54

P

private components model 16
promises
  chaining 128, 130
  common mistakes 132, 133
  parallel execution 131
  used, for dealing asynchronicity 127, 128

R

redo plugin
  developing 121, 122, 123, 124, 127
remote server
  synchronizing 102, 103, 104

S

simple counter example 48
single state tree 20
snapshots 122
stores components model 16
strict mode
  enabling 46

T

test environment
  configuring 62, 63, 64

U

undo plugin
  developing 121, 122, 124, 127

V

View 8
vue-devtools
  Component inspector 106, 107, 108
  Events inspector 109
  installation link 105
  using 105
vue-loader
  used, for single-file components 59, 60
Vue.js reactivity system 22, 24
Vuex applications
  dumb components 91
  smart components 91
Vuex built-in logger plugin
  enabling 112, 113
Vuex framework
  technical requisites 20
Vuex plugin system
  about 115, 116
  technical requisites 115
Vuex store
  about 25
  actions, declaring inside 37
  components' local state 28
  mapState helper 27
  single state tree, accessing inside components
    25